Author:        Glenda Needs

Cover Design:    Courtenay Eckermann

Photography:    Courtenay Eckermann

Published by  InsideArts

Art Therapy: Foundation and Form

ISBN: 978-0-646-57453-0

Format: Paperback

Publication Date: 04/2012  Reprint 01/2013

Recommended Retail Price: $59.00

For more information, please contact

InsideArts PO Box 347, Seacliff Park SA, Australia,  5049

## Acknowledgements

Thank you to the many wonderful people who helped me to overcome my fear of the words and of 'putting pen to paper'.

First I must thank my wonderful daughter Courtenay Eckermann for her beautiful photographs, art work and cover design. She is a remarkable, creative individual.

Thanks to my fabulous husband, Rob, and children, Jaecinta, Courtenay, Bridgette, Sophie, Will and Amelia, who have waited patiently on many occasions whilst 'I just finish this paragraph'. They have provided me with nourishment, news from the outside world, neck massages and encouragement that has kept me going.

Thank you to Sue C and Cath L, my chief content, grammar and spell checkers without whom you'd be struggling through a very different text.

A monster thanks to the amazing Bek B, who amidst her exciting pre-nuptial days completed the arduous task of typesetting and making it all look pretty.

Finally, I want to thank my wonderful Mum and Dad, Harold and Olive, for giving me new pencils and a colouring book almost every Christmas, even though they thought I'd never get to finish it.

www.insidearttherapy.wordpress.com

www.arttherapyaustralasia.com

Table of Contents

# Author's Notes

Throughout this text the use of the words 'problem' and 'issue' refer to the situations that are troublesome for clients. These terms do not in any way reflect on the nature of this situation, nor the value of the person and his/her capacity for healing. Similarly the use of the terms 'client' and 'patient' are literary devices designed to make the communication of the message more fluent and less cumbersome. These terms are not intended to diminish individuality or capacity. The 'therapist' in this text, refers to the Art Therapist.

All case material is a collage of many years of practice and multiple experiences with clients, sprinkled with a little imagination to fill the gaps and demonstrate a point. I respect client confidentiality and will not share individual client stories, nor art work generated during sessions. Although a client may give permission now for such use of his or her story and art work, printed books are around for a long time, and the potential for the client to feel differently about this in the future is certainly possible. All art work included is representative of the art frequently made by clients in such situations.

This text is aimed at providing basic, introductory knowledge regarding the use of art in therapy. It is not a complete instruction manual, nor does it provide adequate knowledge for people to consider themselves, or practice as, an Art Therapist. This text only discusses the Art Therapy for one-to-one therapeutic work for adults with a capacity to understand metaphor. Many of the concepts will be equally applicable for groups, diverse individual clients, and for clients with disabilities. These clients however, will need somewhat of a specialised approach and greater exploration than this text permits. Many other good Art Therapy texts are available for diverse client groups.

The term for art medium is pluralised as 'mediums' to avoid confusion with other popularised forms of the term 'media'.

This text frequently refers to the unconscious. I will not debate the nature of the unconscious here. Whether the unconscious is truly a source of ordered, hidden knowledge or merely a melting pot of experience is irrelevant. It is when the owner of this unconscious makes decisions or interpretations of what he or she sees that is invaluable. When a client sees a teapot in the cloud it may not be a secret message from the unconscious, but of all the possibilities this is what was seen, rather than a cat, a scarf or other object. What caused the client's mind to give the teapot preference over the other objects? The teapot itself may be irrelevant as an object, but what the client does, in creating meaning for this symbol's presentation, is indeed relevant and precious in therapy.

Thank you.

# Foreword

Visual representations of reality i.e, "Art" - for instance, cave paintings and use of sun/moon symbols - have predated written and verbal recorded histories. It makes sense then to use these representations to clarify our internal and external experience, and attempt some reconciliation, or even establish a conversation between the two, using these visual symbols.

In my view, one of the myths of my field of psychiatry is that when insight is gained in therapy, change happens. Art Therapy's first task is to seek an attainment of insight through doing, and using modalities with fewer limitations than words. The use of tactile, kinaesthetic, visual as well as auditory senses seems however to be logical and rich ground to bring about more than just insight; to also bring about growth and change.

Art Therapy research is increasingly validating the use of art as therapy. Art Therapy is clearly a relationship in which the practitioner has one foot in the world of mystery and creativity, and the other in the real world challenges a client brings.  The ability to maintain this space where the therapy can occur is a real skill.  The art therapist needs to have a thorough and confident understanding of the tools that are used. A well-developed and intimate relationship with the art, the media, and the approach is essential.  This text provides a basis for beginning that journey.

I have known Glenda a number of decades and the therapeutic tools she uses mirror her own personal and professional development. Starting with the "fuzzy" and moving to "detail" and "cut out", starting new pictures, or even working on 2 or 3 pictures at once, reflect Glenda's personal and professional development.

When Glenda talks of her work, people lean forward - they want to engage in her story and her story-telling and imagery. It is not surprising that this journey of engagement has expanded with her writing and formalizing her approach. (I hear Glenda in my head, saying, "Yes, but not to be limited by any approach").

Glenda, in her work, is invited into the "created space" of her clients. In writing this book she invites the reader to share the space created by her ideas. This sharing of space is a privilege, demands energy and engagement, but leads to enlightenments, insights and actions that can lead to change in the practice of the reader.

In ending this foreword I am still struck by the humorous paradox of Glenda being frustrated by the limitations of the written word to explain her visual passion. What more fitting statement can one make of an art therapist?

Dr. Malcolm St James (Psychiatrist)

# Preface

I discovered the therapy in art as just a little girl. I spent around two-thirds of my life in hospital before I was aged 12. Every year my parents were told it would be my last. I had been unwell from just a few weeks of age but despite the doom and gloom, I lived on. There were of course days and, indeed many weeks that were difficult. I was frequently isolated in an oxygen tent, viewing the world through murky plastic and in the presence of a permanent hum. I was mostly attached to an intravenous drip, so my 'pole' was my best buddy. I didn't play. Mostly I couldn't play. But I did draw. Lots.

If today's psychologists and psychiatrists were to see some of my drawings I'm sure they'd have predicted I would turn out to be someone very different than I am today. I am certain though that all of this drawing was my psychological saving grace. My art gave me an opportunity to express frustration, confusion, anger, and fear. It also gave me an opportunity to make some meaning of what was happening to me, to express joy, to give something to others, and to play in the only way I knew how.

Thankfully, medical science and my will to live were always just one step ahead of my doctors' determination that I would die. Finally by my late twenties I was told I might get to live to be 100. So I am here, still visiting the doctors too often and sometimes having to curb my enthusiasm for doing things, but my plan is to hang around for a lot longer yet. I have things to do. Like writing a book or two.

After I realised I could finally have a future, I spent many years working at jobs that I wasn't sure I really liked. I then discovered Art Therapy and spent 11 years at university, while again defying the odds and giving birth to and raising six children. I persevered through many late night assignments, sleepless nights with teething babies and even a particularly bad bout of mastitis at exam time, as I truly believed in my chosen career. I knew from personal experience the incredible value in art making. So I kept at it and finally established my own Art Therapy practice.

In the not too distant past, Art Therapy, particularly in South Australia, was a lonely business. I have been practicing Art Therapy for 15 years, yet for many, felt as if I were sailing alone in a wide and dangerous sea. In the earlier days, I battled to secure recognition for my skills, often experiencing a rising frustration at being called the 'craft lady' and having helpful volunteers 'fixing' my client's artwork and giving unsolicited advice for the client's troubles. I had the odd psychiatrist laugh me off. Back then, I also struggled to describe and justify what it was that I did. I couldn't possibly explain how it worked. I just knew that it did.

Necessity deemed that I would have to educate every potential employer, referrer or organisation that dared to give me a moment to speak. They mostly knew nothing about Art Therapy or the potential benefits for clients. I was frustrated by the lack of clarity and simplicity in resources describing Art Therapy. I needed an hour for a full discourse, or had to provide some 'flaky' five-minute description of something that I knew confidently was not 'flaky'.

Over some months, while battling for enough paid work, I developed several presentations, from very small elevator statements to professional presentations and dinner party conversations. I spent a great deal of time researching and uncovering more scientific exploration of what I knew innately, and then in finding the words to describe it.

The process I began then has been infinitely valuable. Every time I launched into my statements I subtly altered them, honed them, and in doing so began to understand more about how to word my chosen passion and profession.

Every year, for every audience, and now in my teaching, the material I present continues to evolve. I add new ideas and research. I draw on my other studies and all of the learning opportunities life presents to better understand the power of art in therapy. It seemed that all this preparation could fill a book, and indeed it does. Despite years of practice and many days of meeting brick walls, I have never lost my passion for Art Therapy. I believe in it. Completely.

Nowadays, there are so many terrific Art Therapy texts and so many wonderfully skilled and knowledgeable Art Therapy practitioners worldwide that one might wonder why I would write a book - especially as I far prefer to paint. Words are not my first language; art is. In my years of teaching I have learnt what many students and new graduates seek are simple descriptions, clear instructions, and the fundamentals laid out in order.

This text is for students and newly graduated Art Therapists, although others may also find it useful. The focus is simple, "What is Art Therapy?" and "How do I actually do it?" Of course, this book alone will not make you an Art Therapist, but if you are seeking some basic understanding of the role of an Art Therapist and you want to make sense of the power in art, then you will find it here. I have not attempted to describe all there is to Art Therapy, as this would require many volumes and much greater knowledge than just mine. Nor can the model I have presented be considered definitive. This text is a start - a strong beginning upon which to build new knowledge and experience.

The material is divided primarily into two parts, with the theory component first and the practical activities second. Many of the topics will end with an experiential task to explore the concepts discussed. Many will also include some suggested further reading. These texts do not necessarily refer to the chapter directly, but will allow you to stretch your thinking further in related fields. Some chapters will include an experiential task and a reading, and others, none.

To fully utilise this book, please prepare yourself with an art book, some simple art materials, a notebook, pen and an enquiring mind. As you generate art from each of the experiential tasks, date and title it. In some instances you will return to this work. Use the notebook to respond to and journal your experiences. This will build a great resource where you can include definitions of terms and further ideas that are generated.

As a therapist, remember self-care is paramount. Please be sure to access regular supervision, whether or not your workplace mandates it. Be sure to take care when completing the experiential tasks, and seek further Art Therapy, counselling, or support if you find an activity has caused wounds to open, or new challenges to appear.

So it's time to begin. Remember, this is an Art Therapy book and doodles or notes in the margins are encouraged.

## Janet and The Cat

Art Therapy:

allows a person to step out of the frame of the prevailing circumstance and in doing so, the art becomes a reflection of the artist's world, assumptions and beliefs.

This process of "stepping out" of the frame, of full externalisation, creates an unknown field, with which the artist now has to be reconciled.

"What do I see?"

The incongruity bellows loudly.

What results is the opportunity for a new way of knowing or a new way of being, never before known to the artist.

It is a creative act. A brave act of trial and error and great invention: the invention of a new self, one never seen before.

When the art therapist first began her practice, she frequently espoused that art therapy did not require words in order to facilitate healing. So understandably, a wise practitioner who was working with a young voluntarily mute woman decided to refer her to the art therapist. This woman had become voluntarily mute since experiencing some frightening bullying in her workplace.

As she was newly graduated, still finding her feet, and eager for some challenging work and income, the art therapist graciously accepted the referral whilst quietly berating herself for making such outrageous claims. Intellectually, she was quite sure that indeed the art would provide the healing, but in reality it had been impossible to find such clients to practice with and so she felt completely unprepared and inadequate. Although she often repeated the 'art does not need words' mantra, she had never actually facilitated therapy without them!

The client, Janet, had a developmental disability and worked full time in a small organisation doing many tasks from photocopying and mail-outs to cleaning the staff room. She had happily worked in the role for four years before gradually becoming increasingly unhappy, finally refusing to attend work and ultimately refusing to speak. In the months prior she had made some claims of bullying that were dismissed as 'usual workplace shenanigans'.

At the first art therapy appointment, Janet seemed extremely passive. Her only acknowledgement that the therapist had even spoken was made by just slightly extending the time of eye contact. The therapist was daunted as she was unsure of Janet's capacity to understand abstract concepts, and just whether the language she used would be appropriate. A support person had offered to attend with Janet, but as she was not comfortable speaking to anyone, the therapist decided that the therapeutic relationship might have a better chance if they could be alone.

The therapist explained to Janet that she would ask her to do things and that Janet could simply comply if she wished. The therapist explained that if Janet did not engage, then she would suggest something else. Janet understood that the therapist knew some of what had occurred. Unless Janet let her know differently, the goal for working together was for Janet to feel happier again, and feel comfortable talking to people. The therapist made a point of assuring her that she wouldn't be pressuring her to talk at all, that she could do so if, and when, she was ready. Janet eyed the therapist quite suspiciously, but maintained a physical position indicative that she was willing to engage.

The therapist spread two sheets of paper in front of them both and chose some chunky crayons to begin. Janet was offered the box to choose a crayon. The therapist chose a colour for herself and began drawing a large continuously looped figure eight on the page. The therapist suggested that Janet try making this art also. After a few minutes of observation, Janet picked up a red crayon and copied the therapist. As she was drawing the therapist spoke about how this exercise can be very relaxing. She went on to say that the rhythm is often soothing and demonstrated how the shape can be formed synchronously with our breathing. The therapist also explained how they could form a pattern on the page through a conscious effort, but could also let go and just trust the body to create the pattern. Janet was asked to close her eyes when she was ready and to just keep looping the figure eights. This art could be thrown away if she wished, and there was no 'right' way to do it.

Janet eventually trusted herself enough to close her eyes and keep the loops flowing onto the page. She peeked, reassured herself, and closed her eyes again. The therapist continued making the art herself, keeping the sound of crayon scratching across the paper as a constant regulator of the timing of the act. As the therapist slowed down, so did Janet. When the therapist stopped, Janet stopped shortly after.

This activity was concluded by encouraging Janet to trust her body and her instincts throughout the art therapy sessions.

The therapist was reluctant to use the art to directly address Janet's inability or unwillingness to talk, as this appeared as a symptom of the problem, not the problem itself. In fact, the muteness was really a protective and healing technique for her in probably the only way she knew how. To do battle with the muteness would simply expose her to more traumas as she became vulnerable again without it.

As a result of this concern, the therapist instead asked Janet if she could draw a shape and colour that could show her level of happiness right now. She was asked to think about the paper being her whole self, right now, and to consider how much of it was happy.

The therapist placed a torso-sized page in front of Janet. If the problem were big enough to cause such a response in her body, a letter size paper would certainly not be adequate. If Janet were to have an oversized page, it may have given concrete form to the problem as if it was much bigger than her, and this could have been quite overwhelming. As the therapist was unsure about Janet's ability to understand the symbolism she further explained. She asked if the happiness was perhaps blue or yellow or red. She asked if it was a smooth ball or a jagged shape.

Janet picked up an orange chalk pastel from the box she was offered and she began to colour diagonally from the bottom right hand corner, to the top right hand corner. The therapist wondered if Janet hadn't understood, until she picked up a purple pastel, and drew a small heart in the bottom right hand corner, and coloured it in with some areas of orange still showing through.

Janet pushed the artwork toward the therapist. The therapist picked the artwork up and shook off the chalk dust. Janet took a sharp inward breath. "Oh! I'm sorry, was the chalk dust important there?" Janet didn't reply, but intuitively the therapist offered the artwork back and Janet again took an orange pastel and created the necessary dust.

The therapist cleared the area around the artwork and asked Janet "Is this a picture of how happy you are now?" Janet did not respond. The therapist floundered. The first rule of art therapy was to never assume anything. She would need to assume that this art was an accurate representation of Janet's level of happiness at the moment. The therapist also recognised her own failure to stand by her earlier commitment to not expect Janet to talk.

Janet gave the therapist a long, intent gaze. It was as if she was challenging the therapist to keep going in spite of having no reassurances from her.


In a moment of panic, the therapist wondered again if she had made a huge mistake and thought perhaps she should admit her inadequacies, make her apologies to Janet and let her go on home.

Then she thought about Janet. She realised that something had locked Janet into her own world, externally silent, but probably bubbling over with an internal dialogue that somehow reinforced her need to stay silent. The therapist thought about what other help might be available for Janet and realised that unless she, the well trained and generally confident art therapist wouldn't help her client express her pain, who would? Janet's only chance of being heard in a way that she could communicate was through the art. The therapist decided transparency was her only hope of getting through this.

"Janet", she began, "I feel sure that something has made you very sad, so sad that you feel you cannot talk. As I said before, this is fine. I just need to let you know, that I believe the art we do here will help you find some more happiness, but I am afraid that I will forget that you aren't talking. I will sometimes need a moment to think about what we can do, or how I am going to help you without expecting you to talk. I want you to know that I might make mistakes, but I will do my very best." Janet held the therapist's gaze and a slight sad smile flittered across her face and quickly faded. Without any other reassurance, the therapist chose to understand this to be acceptance and approval.

The therapist asked Janet to think about something that had made her sad. Janet was asked to draw some of this story on the page. "Janet, you can use symbols, like a box for something that is hidden away inside you, or you can use real pictures, like people, animals, and cars, or you can use colours and shapes that remind you of what happened. Anything is fine"

Again the therapist placed a torso-sized page in front of Janet and, after a pause, she began to work.

Janet drew a simple cat. Around it she drew a box, and finally she coloured it over with a brown crayon and a green line across the top. The therapist, trained to not assume anything about a person's art, could do nothing else but guess the story that the image represented. Janet looked at the image and a tear welled. "I think I can guess what has happened here. I think a cat you loved died. I also think when I look at you that this has made you sad. It's ok to cry here. I have tissues and no one but me will see you." After a few minutes and great determination not to cry, Janet lifted the picture and placed it against her stomach. The therapist offered the client a beautiful envelope with a gold tipped edge for Janet to take away the image, but Janet did not pick it up.

"Perhaps you'd like to remember a beautiful time with the cat instead of the sad time when you had to say goodbye. You can use this page here to draw a time that was lovely if you like". Janet folded the first image and put it under her jumper. She pulled the empty page close and began drawing a sun and a simple garden scene. Janet took a pencil and drew a shape on the grass. At first the therapist believed she was trying to draw a cat, but as Janet used the eraser to rub it out again and again, she understood the image intended was a person. The therapist asked Janet if she would like some help. Janet pushed the page to the therapist and gave her the pencil. Cautiously, always keeping an eye on her client, the therapist did a simple outline of a person sitting on the grass. As the therapist paused to consider her next step, the client pulled the page back to herself. Janet drew a cat in the lap of the person, and began to cry. As the tears subsided, the therapist asked Janet to look for something in the studio that she might like for the picture - an envelope, a frame, a special box, or some stickers. Janet chose a beautiful frame and together they mounted the image and framed it.

As they viewed their handiwork, Janet briefly smiled. The first session was over.

At the next session, Janet helped herself to paper and a packet of markers. The therapist watched as Janet drew another image. There were no tears, but a very firm set mouth and furrowed brow. Janet seemed angry. The picture this time appeared to be about a house, perhaps her own home. A stick person stood outside the home with a very sad looking face. The therapist asked Janet if she would like to create another image that helped her feel better. Janet took a fresh page, but did not begin to draw. She pulled her original back in front of her and placed her hands over the image of the house. Janet was not happy with it and took a blue marker and placed a large cross over the house. After a few moments of contemplation, she again pulled the fresh sheet in front of her and began to draw another house, but with different colour and some different features. Before completing this image, she pulled the old image back again. The therapist said to Janet that she could do whatever she wanted with the image, not just draw with it. She could cut it, fold it, tear it or glue things to it. Janet held the first image thoughtfully before she roughly tore the page between the house and the stick figure. She seemed very angry, and not at all the passive individual she had been the week before. Janet rested her elbows on the table and put her chin in her hands. It seems that this action with the art didn't suit her either. Janet's eyes darted around the room, apparently searching for something. The therapist asked Janet to walk around and look for anything she wanted. Janet found her way to a shelf and collected a roll of tape. Back in her chair, Janet reattached the torn pieces. She then carefully folded the taped up image of the house under the stick figure and again contemplated her work. Finally she took another marker and turned the face of the stick figure into a happy face. Janet clearly wanted this, but found it difficult to create. The therapist offered another round of paper and a glue stick if she wished to recreate this face and glue it over the other, which she accepted.

After satisfactorily completing the artwork and standing back to view it, a huge sigh escaped Janet.

Her anger had abated and she seemed resolved to the story. In some way, she seemed to have made peace with the circumstance she was depicting.

As Janet was leaving, she leaned in to give the therapist a hug. The therapist, momentarily taken aback, recognised this as Janet's means of saying thank you and appropriately entered into the embrace.

Later that afternoon, the therapist pondered how she had been useful for Janet at all. She didn't say or do anything, she hadn't offered appropriate mediums, nor had she reinforced the goal, or directed the activity. Janet seemed to understand the purpose of the art unlike any of the therapist's other clients, and had used it intentionally herself. She suspected that some cognitive shift had occurred for Janet through the art making, but the therapist felt quite superfluous.

The third session began quite tentatively. The therapist had expected that Janet would again direct her own process, but this was not so. Janet sat passively whilst the therapist revisited the goal of helping Janet find happiness again by working through the challenges that she had experienced. The therapist asked Janet to think about the thing that most stopped her from being happy and then asked her to create an image about this in chalk pastel.

After some quiet reflection and a few sighs, Janet slowly began to draw. She drew a number of stick figures on the outside edge of the page, all with sad faces, and some with eyebrows that made them look quite angry. In the centre were a rock-like shape and a cat. Janet spent a great deal of time on this image and was close to tears on a number of occasions.

Once the image was complete, the therapist explained that there was not a lot of time left but that Janet could do something with the image that would help her to feel better about it. Janet rose, and walked to the door to leave. The therapist explained again but Janet seemed determined to leave. Previously Janet had taken her artwork with her, but this time she left it on the table. Janet again leant in to give the therapist a hug.

Again the therapist was plagued with doubts about her ability to help this client. She knew she needed to trust the art process, and wait for any opportunities to present where she could more purposefully use the art. But this was difficult.

At the next session, the therapist left Janet's picture at the end of the table. She first offered for Janet to put this art in the bin, a container, or the filing cabinet or to put it with her coat and bag to take home later that day. Janet did not take up any offer. Before the therapist could frame an approach for the day's work, Janet reached for the paper and the chalk pastels and recreated the drawing of the previous week. Again, Janet was near tears at several points in the process. And again, as soon as she had completed the image Janet left, but not before she gave the therapist a hug. The therapist examined both images for clues and differences, but she could find nothing of significance.

Over the next 8 weeks, each session was the same. Nothing changed. And yet, Janet's support person reported small positive changes in her behaviour.  The therapist was concerned that she was inappropriately continuing her service for this client, and yet she also knew that Janet was capable of using the art for self-reflection and healing as she had done in the first few weeks.  She also couldn't ignore that something was happening.

At the next session, the therapist jumped in before Janet had even sat down and asked if she would start with something different.  The therapist brought out the very first image of the measure of happiness.  This was the orange page with a tiny purple heart. Again the therapist asked Janet if she could draw a shape and colour that could show her level of happiness right now.  She was asked to think about the paper being her whole self, right now after the work they had done together, and to consider how much of it was happy.  Janet looked carefully at the image she had created previously before she began.  Janet again covered the page in orange, but with less care to cover the entire white page and with less pressure on the pastel.  When she drew the purple heart, Janet examined the first drawing closely and made it slightly larger with intent.  The therapist placed the pages next to one another and commented that she could see some changes.  Janet smiled fleetingly.  Janet was then asked to create another image, one that showed just how much happiness she thought she could have. The therapist noted for her that everyone has some sadness and challenge in their lives and usually some happiness too.  She wondered aloud how much happiness Janet thought she could have, was it more than now?  What was the best Janet thought it could be?

Again, Janet covered the page in orange, but very loosely and then added a purple heart almost two-thirds the size of the page.  The therapist then explained that this picture is the purpose of the art therapy - to assist Janet to reach that level of happiness. "Let's try it, shall we?" asked the therapist.  "What is getting in the way, or stopping you from being this happy Janet?"

The therapist placed another page in front of Janet.  To the therapist's amazement, Janet again drew the same image she had completed many times before, that of the stick persons, the rock like shape and the cat.  But this time there was a small but noticeable difference.  The rock shape had smoothed out somewhat, and had become elongated. The therapist pointed this out to Janet and she seemed surprised.

At the next four sessions Janet again drew the same image, but the rock like shape had morphed.  It had slowly become smooth, elongated and light coloured.   Janet viewed the image, looked at the therapist and with no hesitation or hint of indecision said "I want to tell you what this is".  In that moment the therapist froze. Should she acknowledge what had just occurred? Should she minimize this momentous occasion? Janet noticed the therapist's shock, pause and slight smile, and in acknowledgement dropped her chin and smiled at the table. Her smile faded quickly and she began to cry. "It is an egg," she said...and not another word.

Over the following sessions, Janet drew the egg slowly cracking open. The cat disappeared from the image, and eventually another stick figure emerged from the egg. Over another two sessions the central stick figure grew and developed a wide smile. The other stick figures became smaller, less featured in the image. Their features were blurred. The artistic energy was spent on the central image. Janet began to talk. Initially she spoke just simple phrases containing essential information; slowly moving into more general communication about the sessions and her wider life.

Janet shared some of the experiences that had stolen her happiness. She spoke about how she felt that the therapist was 'listening' to her. She spoke how the mean people in the art weren't as mean as she first thought, and she told the therapist of a few things that had helped. But the one thing that really worked? "I got tired of being a rock," she said.

## What Is Art Therapy?

"We should not pretend to understand the world only by the intellect: we apprehend it just as much by feeling. Therefore, the judgement of the intellect is, at best, only the half of truth, and must, if it be honest, also come to an understanding of its inadequacy." (Jung, 1921)

"The dynamic principle of fantasy is play, a characteristic also of the child, and as such it appears inconsistent with the principle of serious work. But without this playing with fantasy no creative work has ever yet come to birth. The debt we owe to the play of imagination is incalculable. It is therefore short-sighted to treat fantasy, on account of its risky or unacceptable nature, as a thing of little worth" (Jung, 1921)

To define Art Therapy, we must first grapple with that slippery definition of 'art'. 'Art' is a relatively new name for objects or actions considered functional in ancient societies. Greek theatre was considered 'cathartic', decorated potteries in some cultures were designed to appease the gods, and many sculptures and decoration were used to signify importance. All of these we may now consider art.

A better definition of art might be one that highlights the process of an artist in developing a product. Thus art might be defined as the product of skill and originality in the creation of objects, activities, environments, or experiences that are representations of the imaginings of the creator.

'Therapy' is a word with vast application in the English language. We now have Occupational Therapists, Speech Therapists, Psychotherapists, and Aroma Therapists to name just a few. The overarching definition of therapy is perhaps that it is a health professional's practice that aims to provide remedial or compensatory assistance to improve function or wellbeing.

Thus Art Therapy could be defined as the act of creating original products that are representations of the imaginings of the creator that in turn improve function and wellbeing. Really, what the client seeks in Art Therapy is to feel better.

Most Art Therapists are likely to define the profession as a skill set and approach that enables and facilitates an individual or group to create positive outcomes in their lives through the use of an artistic medium and expression.

This therapy may occur through many means but this book will focus largely on the two most common methods - incidental and directed methodologies. Therapy can also occur through other means, for instance, in the witnessing of great works of art, or through documenting societal oppression and freedoms through art making. These models will also be more easily understood when some of the basics of how art influences the psyche is revealed. Of course, there is much we do not understand about how art 'works'. We must hold onto that often repeated request to 'trust the process'.

In incidental Art Therapy, the therapy occurs as a result of engaging in an art process. Many will understand the value in simply engaging fully in art making or creativity of some kind. At times, this activity has almost trance like qualities, a full immersion into the world of the art whilst the temporal everyday world slips away. My father-in-law would paint for hours, oblivious to the phone ringing, people knocking on the front door, and his need for food and drink. As a result he would return to the temporal world, rested, re-energised and excited about his experiences. My own experience is a little less impressive. As I paint, I can often feel the world slipping away, and although I will hear the telephone as it jolts me back to reality, I may also work for an hour or two oblivious to the passage of time, finally looking up at the clock to discover that what seemed like only twenty minutes, was actually a three hour process. I too, feel refreshed and more centred after my time immersed in the art. This is the simplest form of incidental therapy. Many people experience this, perhaps even whilst gardening, sculpting, sewing, playing an instrument or doing mosaics.

In directed Art Therapy the therapist will work with the client's goals, facilitating and supporting him or her to explore, find insight and resolution for an issue by carefully selecting the mediums, the tasks and the conditions under which this therapy occurs. The therapist will choose paper and a medium to resonate with or challenge the client's experience. The therapy may also involve a meditation or guided visualisation.

The therapist will pose a specific question or task to direct the art making and will then provide techniques to thoroughly examine the art for further insight. Eventually, the art will be used to confirm new ways of being, or new knowledge.

Art Therapists can use any methodology along the incidental-directed continuum. It is rare that a purely incidental, or fully directed method would be used, but more likely that it would tend to one or the other end of this continuum. The therapist, regardless of where he or she generally practices within this continuum, will still move up and down the scale to some degree in every session, adapting the approach to the immediate needs of the client or client group, the goal in therapy and the task at hand. Early sessions will often be based in more incidental outcome, until the therapeutic relationship develops and trust is established.

Of course, many people use art therapeutically. Artists and therapists working in community centres with groups of people brought together by common experience may conduct art making sessions with the sole purpose of having the participants feel connected and supported, allowing them to feel heard, and for the pain and joy to be shared. This work is often extremely beneficial for the participants. The persons conducting these art-based programs may or may not be Art Therapists. Artists are often employed in such roles and frequently the reported outcomes are as valuable as the outcomes from those groups facilitated by Art Therapists.

There are however, a number of valuable additional skills that an Art Therapist brings to this style of program. An Art Therapist will focus less on the final product, or the aesthetics, and will support and draw attention to the value in participating, in the art making itself, and the insights, friendships and outcomes attained. An Art Therapist will also be aware of the many challenges in working with marginalised or at risk groups. The Art Therapist will be alert to many indicators, including potential re-traumatisation, resistance, denial, and the group dynamics that can be a microcosm, or a smaller representation of how the participants might operate in the larger societal realm. The design of the program itself can be modified and to some extent directed by the Art Therapist, who can respond to the emerging needs of the participants. In the event of a participant entering into an emotional experience that is to be healthily expressed and witnessed, the Art Therapist can safely support this person through the process.

Directed Art Therapy requires the skills of trained Art Therapists. In this instance, the entire course of the art process is strongly directed to serve the client's goal. For instance, if a client wishes to complete the grieving over a lost relationship, to heal and move on, then each art activity and the reflection process will work with or address an element of this story. The Art Therapist brings expertise that allows him or her to facilitate work that best provides access to healing. For instance, the client's initial 'fuzzy understanding of what went wrong in the relationship' would be contained on a page no bigger than the client's torso, to allow a full expression of the experience, but without this situation being represented as 'beyond them' or bigger than the client's power or capacity to deal with it.

It is quite likely that the Art Therapist will ask the client to use a 'fuzzy' medium, for instance soft chalky pastel. This medium is 'fuzzy' in itself, it is difficult to make fine detail, and the tendency is for the medium here to blend and smudge. This response by the Art Therapist is creating resonance with the client's experience. To use felt tip markers for such a task would be considered a challenge to the client's experience of the fuzziness. However markers may be used further into the process when the client wishes to express something very clear and concrete that is useful in attaining the therapeutic goal. The therapist offers these in line with his or her knowledge, the experience of resonance and the myriad of possible paths to healing for each individual client.

The art itself is healing, and sometimes quite insightful, but it is in the skilfully facilitated deeper engagement with the art making process that greater efficacy can be found. Art Therapy is not just talk therapy with art, but something far more complex and intriguing.

The Art Therapist would also bring a vast array of techniques that can be used to further develop a client's understanding and awareness. For instance, after completing the art work and the 'processing' (a term used to describe the way in which the art is then explored and which will be further explained in later chapters), the client may have identified an area in the original image where greater detail is present and where the client knows some of the causes for the relationship breakdown. To further explore this, the Art Therapist may ask the client to enlarge this area of the artwork to reveal more detail. Alternatively, if the client frequently used the verbal expression 'I think I know what is behind this', the Art Therapist may ask the client if he or she would like to cut a window through the page, to another paper behind, and to create the 'what is behind'. There are a vast number of possibilities for the Art Therapist to build richness into the art experience.

Thus we can see that the therapy may occur at either end of the spectrum, through the incidental value of art making, or the directed work facilitated by an Art Therapist.

This text aims to explore some of the many basic skills a competent Art Therapist would possess. Of course, one would not read a book about physiotherapy and assume the position of expert, nor call themselves physiotherapists. Similarly, Art Therapists need extensive experiential training to be able to respond in the moment, and to intuitively work with whatever the client may bring. Wonderful, but untrained art group facilitators may see powerful outcomes for their clients in art making, but this is not so often the skill of the quasi Art Therapist as it is the power of the art. Counsellors, psychologists and psychiatrists may use art in the 'talking cure', but again this alone does not make it Art Therapy. Just as a caring person administering a gentle neck rub may afford the 'patient' some great benefits, this alone does not make them a physiotherapist!

Art Therapy is a justifiable and evidence based mental health practice. Although many people make art, and experience the wonderful therapeutic qualities of doing so, an Art Therapist brings an intimate knowledge of how colour, shape, metaphor, symbolism and imagery intersect with the deeper psyche and can facilitate great psychological and emotional healing.

Experiential task

Set a timer for 15 minutes. When you have finished, this art piece will be disposed of so no expertise is required. Utilising any drawing or painting materials at hand and a large sheet of art paper, simply surrender yourself to the medium. Create abstract lines and shapes. Totally immerse yourself, do not direct your thinking, and just let it flow. When the timer sounds, continue, but observing yourself, noting what it is about the medium that draws your attention, what is happening in your mind, what feelings arise and where these are in your body.

Stop when you feel the unstructured art is complete. What is this feeling of complete-ness? If you become critical of what you see, stop and ask yourself why the product has become important despite the knowledge that it is to be disposed of and will not be witnessed by others.

Art can be a remarkably soothing act until we turn judgement upon it.

Further Reading

Cathy A Malchiodi, *Handbook of Art Therapy*, 2nd edition, 2011, Guilford Press

Cathy A Malchiodi, *The Soul's Palette: Drawing on Art's Transformative Powers*, 2002, Shambhala

Sharon Soneff, *Art Journals and Creative Healing: Restoring the Spirit Through Self-Expression*, 2008, Quarry Books

# PART ONE   The Science of Art Therapy

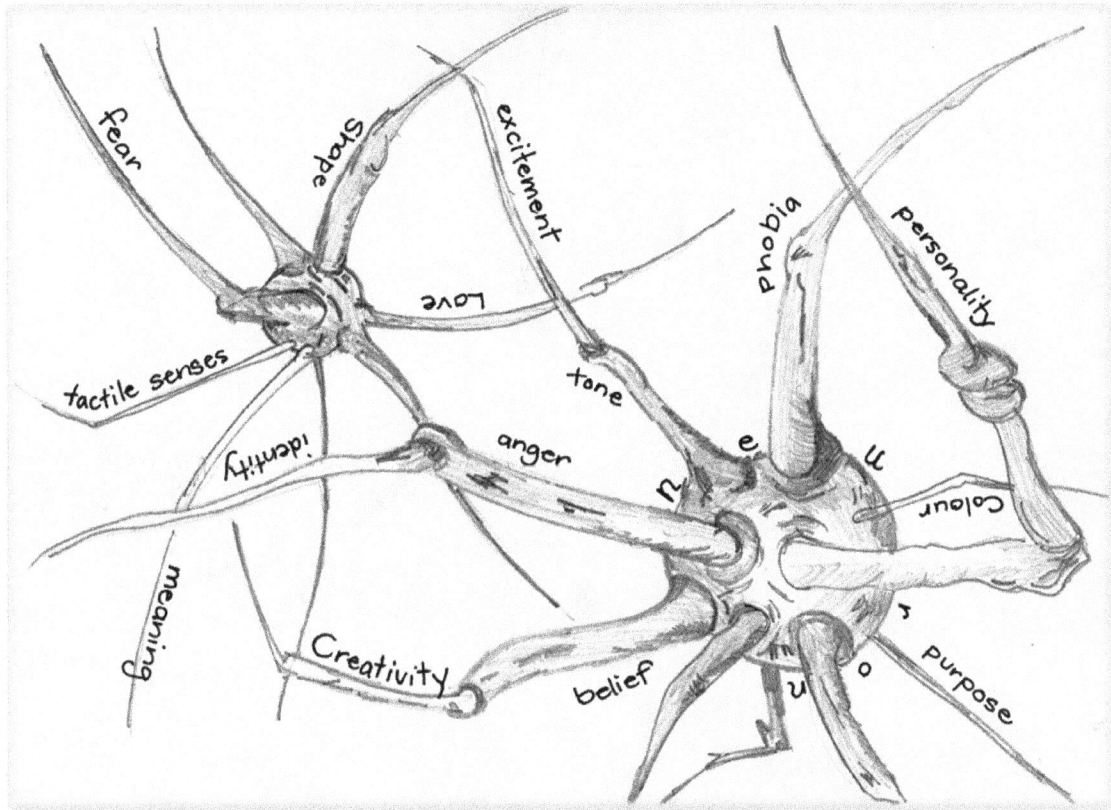

*Art – 'A portion of Me'*

Brains

Although the field of arts therapy has a long history, particularly in the UK and USA, justification for the use of the arts has largely only been through qualitative or anecdotal evidence. Very little research has been directed toward the neurological functions and cognition theories that support the use of arts as an effective therapeutic tool. Verbal counselling relies on the client or learner to verbally construct and reconstruct their personal stories in such a way that provides new insight and the opportunity for growth. Art Therapists incorporate arts mediums into this story telling process in order to engage other senses, access other material and to widen the patients' scope of potentially therapeutic engagement.

Neural network concepts of learning and thinking may provide some understanding to the significance of arts therapy practice as a valuable psychological intervention.

Neural networks models of cognition are simplified models that can explain some of the ways the brain functions. The brain is composed of a large numbers of units (neurons) together with weights that measure the strength of connections (synaptic links) between these units.

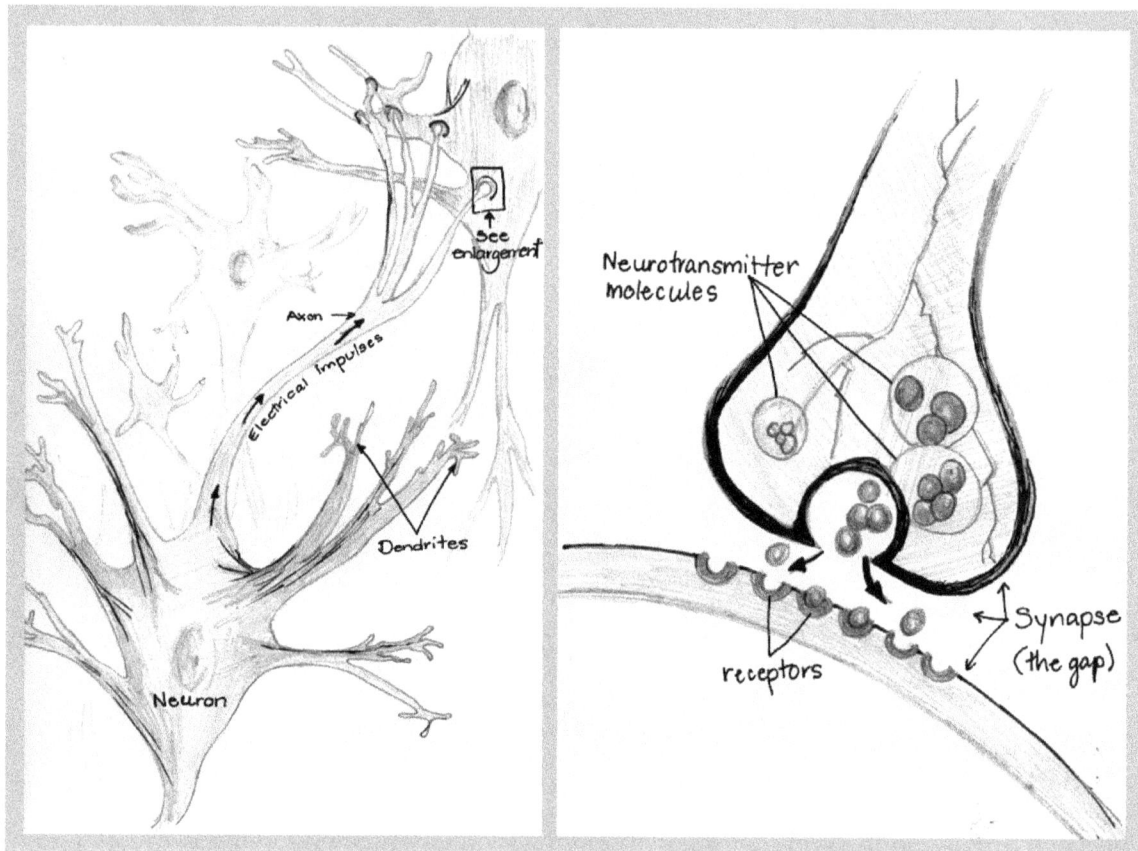

*Neurons and Synaptic Transmission*

Experiments on models of this kind have demonstrated an ability to learn such skills as face recognition, reading, and the detection of simple grammatical structure. This model supposes that psychological challenge and response can also be learned, and with powerful enough detection tools we might even be able to see the trauma laid out in the neural network.

Although the detail in the psychological functioning of an individual is not yet predictable or observable to human examination, we can be assured this information is represented in an ordered and relatively consistent manner for that person. Each experience adjusts neural synaptic connections and activity in ways that are truly unique to each individual, and forms a neurological map, a history and proposals for his or her future.

Following a critical psychological incident, a person attempts to make sense of his experience by following many paths within the neurological map, to understand the incident's place in his or her life and to move forward. How a person responds to a critical incident cannot be easily predicted, and is affected by his or her other personal experiences, beliefs and learning which have formed this neurological map. The sum total of this person's neural synaptic layout is unique because the 'wiring' has been created from prior learning and experience.

Single challenging events do not frequently result in long-term dysfunctional outcomes, but perhaps a repeated combination of experiences can reinforce unhelpful patterns of behaviour and set these within the neurological map. The effect upon the neural network can be described using the analogy of a stone in a pond. In a single stone drop, our ability to predict and respond to the ripples is greater than if a handful of stones are dropped in the same pond in quick succession. In this instance many concentric circles are created that will interact with each other in complex ways. Thus where a single event may create a relatively predictable pattern of neural connections, the sum total of many life events creates a myriad of possibilities, all with a different impact upon the individual's experience and perspective. If we take this analogy further, we can see that where stones have been dropped before, the bed of the pond is irregular, and perhaps the perimeter also. Both the bed and perimeter shape will also affect the nature of the ripples in the pond. To predict how a single incident will impact upon any individual's life and to assume that this will be consistent for all humans is absurd.

Experiential task

Create some sheets of marbled paper. Observe the intricacies within the patterns. Spend a few moments reflecting on your brain's recording of the sum total of your experiences. The intricacies within your neural network are much more complex than those within this marbled piece, and each one is unique. No amount of effort in creating the exact environment in which the first piece of marbling was created could result in a clear replication of the design.

*Every brain is far more unique than a fingerprint.*

Further Reading

Michael S Gazzaniga, *Who's in Charge?: Free Will and the Science of the Brain*, 2011 Ecco

/

Sam Wang and Sandra Aamodt, *Welcome to Your Brain: Why You Lose Your Car Keys but Never Forget How to Drive and Other Puzzles of Everyday Life*, 2008, Bloomsbury

# The limitations of language

The words we use to describe our unique experiences are limited when compared to our ability for sensory discrimination. If we try to verbally describe the taste alone of a cup of coffee, we may struggle to seek out appropriate descriptive words and are unlikely to be successful without utilising visual and culturally appropriate descriptors such as colour, or "the hot drink we have to get us going in the morning". Inadvertently we may describe a cup of tea. But how long does it take us to easily recognise the taste of coffee? Our sensory taste receptors are far more accurate and speedy, with a wider 'vocabulary' than our verbal language. We can know the difference between tastes and understand these sensory messages very quickly without ever having to find words for them.

Even descriptions of everyday events utilise sensory terms. We understand 'warm relationships', 'cold shoulders', 'feeling low' and 'high', having a 'blue day' and when someone can 'see right through us'. The visual sensory system within the brain is able to store a much more accurate description of a face than words can articulate or 'remember'. We look at a face and know it, even if we cannot remember their name!

In Post Traumatic Stress Disorder, physical actions and other sensory matches that occur following the initial incident have much more emotional weight than verbal descriptions of the experience. Often sensory experiences that replicate some aspect of the traumatic experience can re-awaken the initial fear. This occurs less frequently with a verbal recollection of the trauma, but more frequently from an occurrence that reactivates some of the initial trauma's stored sensory memory. Talking about gun fire may be manageable, whereas the sound of a car backfiring may have enough sensory overlap with gunfire that the sound reconnects more sensory aspects of the original trauma and is thus much more difficult to separate from the experience. Utilizing the sensory qualities of a medium in a purposeful way can be extremely powerful. This does mean that any practitioner utilizing a medium in which sensory experience is revisited must be well aware of and cautious not to precipitate re-traumatisation of the client.

For many years visual cueing has been used to help people with Parkinson's disease to walk. Footprints or stripes are used on the floor surface to provide external cueing for the action. Both techniques probably use the central nervous system to compensate for brain deficits. Kinaesthetic feedback and automatic movement are affected in Parkinson's and the visual process can act like a 'back door' to the brain's instructions to the body to move, where perhaps the front door to such instruction is blocked. This effectively places the cueing for an action as externally, rather than internally generated. Visual input uses different circuits in the brain and this is applicable to healthy individuals as well. (Azulaya, Mesureb, & Blin, 2006)

If our lives are recorded in a sensory pattern of neural connections and words do not adequately describe sensory experiences, then engaging a symbolic and multi-sensory model for resolution of an issue will lay a new pathway, and thus new possibilities for healing, in the sensory neural network. Language alone, with limited sensory engagement, may not be the most effective method for changing a well laid down pattern of psychological dysfunction.

Although some of the activity in the brain is 'hardwired', neural network models explain how multiple sensory input can enhance learning and change and create new networks in the neurological map. If psychological therapies are considered learning new patterns of thinking or rationalizing emotive behaviour, then Art Therapy is learning through lived experience and is best facilitated by multi-sensory engagement with one's individual stories.

The field of Arts Therapy is yet to prove underlying positive neurological change as an outcome for this method of psychological intervention. It is still only possible to collect anecdotal evidence and speculate that sensory engagement in psychological therapy better communicates with the cognitive, emotional and somatosensory neural networks and in doing so creates greater efficacy than purely verbal therapy models.

Experiential task

Find yourself a safe space and time to reflect on an experience that you have struggled to find words to adequately describe. Think carefully about a medium in which to express this experience. Does it need to be flowing, solid, silky, precise, moveable or permanent? Give yourself a time limit and create an image using colours, shapes or objects that best sum up this experience.

Prepare a closing 'act' in order to return to your day, leaving behind any unhelpful feelings that are generated in the activity. To do this, ask yourself if there is something you can do to the artwork that will give you a sense of power or control? Perhaps covering the image in some symbolic way will give you closure to the act. Close the art making session with this action.

*How did the art allow expression that was not easily conveyed through verbal communication?*

Further Reading

Mark Turner, *The Literary Mind: The Origins of Thought and Language*, 1998, Oxford University Press

Lois Carey, *Expressive and Creative Arts Methods for Trauma Survivors*, 2006, Jessica Kingsley Publishers

## Justification for art in therapy

Art is so completely embedded in our way of living that we often forget to truly see just how it serves us. People are intrinsically creative. Whether it is solving the problem of finding the right blouse to wear, how to arrange all of the linen in the linen cupboard, or choosing the right doona cover for summer we seem to draw upon some invisible knowing about whether we are 'right' in our choice. And despite many men's protestations that they aren't creative, they too are not immune. Even for those who engage in no formal art or creative pursuit, it is highly likely that he or she will make many choices throughout life that are based on some aesthetic preference.

If it is not in a 'whatever is clean' fashion mantra, perhaps it's the wheel trims for the car, the car seat covers, or the style of executive chair in the office. Women and men may dress in a style that speaks volumes about who they believe themselves to be. People choose a paint scheme and art for their walls, decide if this scarf 'goes' with this outfit, design gardens and homes, play music, dance, doodle, knit or decorate cakes. For most of us we <u>could</u> live our lives not engaging in such an expression of creativity. We <u>could</u> indeed defer every decision to television, advertising or the latest home design magazine. But even so, very few people slavishly follow these trends. Instead we reflect on which of the current styles might 'suit' us best. Thus, we are creative, if not in direct action, at least in preference and choice.

It is as if we are built with an innate desire for aesthetic beauty that is individual and expressed through our choices. Trying to decipher and justify our choices is often fruitless. I choose something because I 'like it'. It appeals to my senses. For this, perhaps I have no words, just a feeling.

Our feelings about what can be considered an art form are also influential and yet poorly justified. I hear many people say that they haven't a 'creative bone in their body'. Yet they too make decisions about their daily life reflecting some type of aesthetic ability, and when asked to draw a simple line drawing of an apple, these people are also quite adept at it.

Take a piece of paper now and spend 20 seconds completing a life size line drawing of an apple. Easy? Or does your apple look more like a cherry, or an orange?

This is a fascinating ability. The line drawing of an apple that was so easily constructed (despite protestations that some people don't have 'artistic bones') is actually only a simple representation of your lived experience of an apple. An apple has weight, colour, three dimensionality, a temperature, texture and so on. The drawing is just lines which share only a few qualities with our lived experience, and many qualities in contradiction of our lived experience. The blue pen line may have roughly the same shape as the apple you know, but the stem and leaves that you may have added, frequently do not appear on the apples we buy at the supermarket. Also the colour of the pen line, and the colour of the page behind, perhaps it is white, is in contradiction to our lived experience of an apple. Yet the image is believable. Others may look at it and without any prompting recognise this as an apple. The 'symbol' is meaningful.

So let's return to this image of the apple. Work some more on your image, making it as believable as possible. Add colour and more lines to make this apple convincing and authentic. Add whatever you need. Take two or three minutes to do so.

Look at your apple now. Of course, you would now recognise that even with the additions it is still only a little like the lived experience of an apple. What did you add? A small area of highlight or a shadow perhaps? Did you darken one edge of the apple to give it a three dimensional appearance? Did you add a worm, or bruises, an imperfection? Did you give it colour, or 'label' it? Did you draw a computer screen around it? (Thanks to Apple computers for being forever in the service of Art Therapy)

Once again, I am certain you will have realised that even adding 'light' is merely a representation of light, and that an imperfection in a highly imperfect representation is a visual oxymoron. Yet the image is somehow more fulfilling of our notion of an apple, even down to the detail of a smiling worm with its head poking out. This collective information adds to the weight of the argument for this object being a representation of an apple. Thus even simple objects, easily created by most people, can be a means of communicating a message.

Take a few moments now to think about the apple in a different way. Imagine this convincing, believable apple as a metaphor for being a convincing, believable human being.

**Some of the ways we might consider this**

Convincing human beings:

- Have a skin colour that can be one of many
- Come in many shapes and sizes
- Are individuals, yet come from a family 'tree'
- Often show evidence of bumps and bruises, not trusting others, being afraid in certain circumstances etc.
- Have both light and shadow in their lives, good times and bad
- Have a 'core'
- Holds the capacity for reproducing itself
- Often grow in relation to the environment in which they were nurtured
- Feel like they have 'had a bite taken out of them'
- Often experience a sense of identity when they have a meaning or context (In a fruit bowl ready for eating or on a computer screen!)
- Occasionally humans get worms!

The process we have just completed is really quite remarkable.  To begin with, you were able to very quickly transfer your lived experience of an apple into a line drawing, with no further instruction and remarkably knowing that if someone else saw this image he too would recognise it.  You were then able to consider what is was to be authentic or believable as an apple, and you again used drawn lines to make it more convincing.  Finally, you were able to use this image and notion of a believable apple as a metaphor for what it is to be a convincing, believable human being, lumps bumps and all. This is an amazing skill that we have as humans, and underlies the basics of art as therapy.

Of course the drawn apple is something of a learned expression.  Our mothers perhaps draw apples for us as children and we know the essential elements.  Books and other media regularly represent apples in such a way.  However not all of this understanding is a learned response.

What appears to happen when we see a cat is that the brain's visual cortex selectively recognizes certain categories of objects, and via the means of elimination quickly determines that this is an animal of a certain species; a cat.  The brain does not need a huge amount of information to do this reductive process, and with cats it appears that initially at least, whiskers, ears and eyes are sufficient for a best guess that an image appears to be a cat, provided no other highly incongruous elements are present (e.g. the cat has an elephant's trunk).

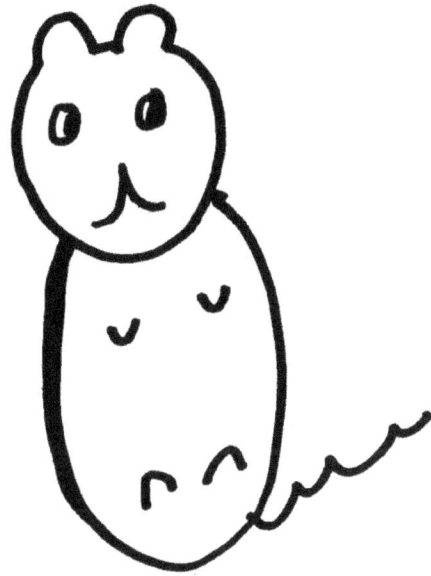

*Is it a cat?*                    *Is it a cat?*

The pattern for reduction in the brain's processing is so strong and consistent that researchers can use mathematical algorithms to find out what a person is viewing just by examining the pattern of neural responses. Interestingly these responses occur regardless of the object's scale or degree of rotation. Remarkably, recognition of an object can be made within as little as 100 milliseconds. (Liu, 2009)

The brain's ability to do a process of elimination and then make a 'best guess' is perhaps why we can recognise very simple objects.

Imagine that you and a friend attended a country fair where a cartoonist took a photograph of your friend and instructed you to return in an hour to collect a caricature. Eventually you return to collect the artwork. As you approach the stall, many caricatures are propped up and and yet you instantly recognise your friend's face amongst them all. At close inspection though, it can be difficult, unless you are a cartoonist, to describe the resemblance. Our brain sees and knows; yet we fail to have words to describe this.

In order to understand this we need to recognise that sensation is not the same as perception. Sensation refers to the input of unregulated sensory data from the external world into the brain. Perception then organizes sensory information into a mental pattern in order to make it meaningful. The mental pattern is then presented to the neurological map, upon which the new information is laid for a match. Failing to find an exact match, the brain will look for the closest match, and integrate this new material into the existing neurological map. We cannot observe ourselves in this process. We merely trust it occurs. This means that when we see a caricature, what we sense is far more accurate that what we can necessarily describe.

Another important factor in our ability to use art therapeutically is our capacity for metaphor. Although as adults we have a vast understanding of worded metaphor, children have an innate capacity to recognise shared qualities, which is the basis for the development of metaphor generally.

Mark Turner, in A Literary Mind, describes shared attributes in early childhood imagination,

"A two-year-old child who is leading a balloon around on a string may say, pointing to the balloon, "This is my imagination dog." When asked how tall it is, she says, "This high," holding her hand slightly higher than the top of the balloon. "These," she says, pointing at two spots just above the balloon, "are its ears." This is a complicated blend of attributes shared by a dog on a leash and a balloon on a string. It is dynamic, temporary, constructed for local purposes, formed on the basis of image schemas, and extraordinarily impressive. It is also what two-year-old children do all day long. True, we relegate it to the realm of fantasy because it is an impossible blended space, but such spaces seem to be indispensible to thought generally and to be sites of the construction of meanings that bear on what we take to be reality." (Turner, 1998)

This ability forms the very earliest use of metaphor – recognition of shared attributes or qualities that enable the child to hold such a concept in an imaginary space, and to create a new story or new possibilities from those attributes. Another example quite pertinent to art therapies, in particular movement therapy is when a child straddles the low pine railing fences that sometimes surround playgrounds. The child then declares to all "See, I am riding a pony". The child understands him or herself in relation to the imagined object – in a physically imagined space. We can imagine ourselves a different world, a different way of being, and the creative act of art making can support this process.

Except for individuals with some significant disabilities, humans generally have the capacity to use imagery and symbols meaningfully, to understand metaphor, and to use the combination of these skills to reflect upon the human condition.

Experiential task

Create an image that resonates with the feelings you are experiencing regarding Art Therapy right now.

What symbols did you use?   In describing this to another, what worded metaphors would you use?

**Further Reading**

Noah Hass-Cohen and Richard Carr, *Art Therapy and Clinical Neuroscience*, 2008, Jessica Kingsley Publishers

Arthur P. Shimamura and Stephen E Palmer, (editors), *Aesthetic Science: Connecting Minds, Brains, and Experience*, 2012, Oxford University Press

## Trusting the senses

As a baby, before we had experiences that we had words for, our memory was still gathering information from the senses, although a great deal of this memory would be lost. The hippocampus is a brain structure thought to be crucially involved in the formation of memory for facts and events. At birth and in very early childhood this structure is not fully grown, and so retaining memory of experiences is unlikely. What is interesting however, is that the brain structure for emotional memory, the amygdala, is mature in infancy. The outcome being that an emotionally significant event in infancy leaves an emotional marker that may affect the way a child behaves later in life despite them not being able to remember the actual event, and certainly not being able to describe the pivotal event as the hippocampus was not present at the time to record such memories.

As a baby begins to develop emotional 'memory' through the amygdala, and as the hippocampus begins to develop and starts to store information, this information is laid down to form the primary neural networks for cognition. This information formed a platform upon which new experiential data was layered and building ways of knowing that was not encoded in words until much later, if ever. Although it is easy to think our world can be fully explained in words, this is actually not so. Our senses make meaning of our world and use this information in decision making every day.

Imagine someone has left the milk out overnight. You can smell it and the milk still seems to be safe to use. You make a cup of coffee, add some sugar perhaps, and then slowly add in some milk. The milk does not curdle, so you are hopeful the coffee will be drinkable. Finally, you take the coffee to your lips, tip slowly and sip, smacking your lips and tongue together to awaken your taste buds and test the freshness of the milk. A few seconds later, you are reassured. You then take a generous mouthful without the attention to detail you applied with the first sip.

What were you doing with the first sip? You very carefully separated out the taste of the coffee, the taste of the sugar and the taste of the milk, and then you tested the milk taste for freshness. Can you word instructions for this task for someone who has no concept of off milk? No. In fact our taste buds have acumen that far outstrips that of our language. We may know the taste of sour milk but can we describe this in taste alone? Do we have words to describe the task for separating out the tastes of the sugar and coffee? We trust our gustatory senses to guide our safe ingestion of food every day, yet we do not have words guiding this.

Much of our day-to-day activity requires just such embodied knowledge. We do not 'think' about walking, we have not cognitively acknowledged the exact temperature when we put on a coat. We do not have words for what occurs to our heart when we fall in love, or for deep sadness. Yet we experience these things. The sensory system is responding, yet we cannot neatly define these responses in words. Our language has convenient phrases such as "words fail me", "I can't talk about it" or even "it's just a gut feeling".

Words are symbols. They are a rough approximation of our experience, captured in words in order to communicate this experience to another. Words are no more or less symbolic of our experience than art can be. They are simply alternative means for different target audiences. Frequently words are for communicating detail to others, whereas art maybe about communicating a sensory message to another. Consider Edvard Munch's "The Scream". This art piece conveys great fear to the viewer in a way that does not define how the viewer generates the fear, but merely the extent of the sensory experience.

Munch himself stated the goal of his art as "the study of the soul, that is to say the study of my own self" (Faerna, 1995)

In describing what led to this painting Munch describes a sensory and symbolically rich impetus,

"I was walking down the road with two friends when the sun set; suddenly, the sky turned as red as blood. I stopped and leaned against the fence, feeling unspeakably tired. Tongues of fire and blood stretched over the bluish black fjord. My friends went on walking, while I lagged behind, shivering with fear. Then I heard the enormous, infinite scream of nature." (Prideaux, 2005)

Empathy depends upon the brain's capacity to simulate a response expected to be present in the sensory system of another. When we see someone who is sad and empathise, we instruct our sensory system to be sad also, merely separating the final cognitive aspect of who owns the initial sadness. We enter into a similar sensory experience as the other, but we further cognise that it is not ours to own. Munch's painting, without words, powerfully allows us to experience something of his despair.

Clearly in discussions on Art Therapy, our visual system is paramount. It is also necessary to examine how much reliability we place upon our visual system.

Every moment with our eyes open we develop perceptions about the world and operate our visual tasks with considerable ease - we somehow find our car keys in a mess on the hall table; we drive on busy roadways; we recognize familiar faces in a crowd; and as we grow up we learn the difference between cats, chairs and lizards even though they all have four legs!

We have an unshakeable belief that we "see" the world—that the images in our mind are the accurate reflection of an external reality. Actually this is an elaborate story. For example, there is no colour in the world around us; there are simply surfaces that reflect various wavelengths of light. Despite this we perceive colour in vivid detail and in the mere microseconds of time. We have only a limited understanding of the mechanisms underlying vision and the brain's work in turning the work of the eye into meaningful material for us to use. Despite this, we do know that the visual sense, and indeed all senses can de 'directed'. We can select to divert our attention away from the peripheral, immediately unnecessary sensory material collected, and focus on that which best serves us.

For instance, our eye collects an enormous amount of data. Our peripheral vision collects as much data as our central vision, yet we see what we intend to see, or where our attention is focussed. At this moment, my attention is focussed on my keyboard and screen, yet in my peripheral vision the door, window and one wall of my study are visible. A bird may fly past my window, yet I would be unlikely to notice it. In fact, a gorilla may press its face to my window and I may not 'see' it. My eyes will collect the data, yet my brain will dispose of this particular information before it reaches my awareness as I have thoroughly directed my awareness towards my current task in writing this text. Although now, I am feeling a bit stretched and scatty, my attention is so diffuse that I am finding it hard to concentrate on the keyboard and task at hand. I have now broadened my scope of attention to much more within my visual field.

This selected attention does not only apply to the visual system. It is the technique we used in the example of selecting the milk for scrutiny in the example given earlier. It is also a process that occurs within our auditory system.

Imagine standing with a small group of friends at a party. The music is playing loudly in the background; others are talking, singing or perhaps shouting around you. Your ears 'hear' all of the sounds yet your attention is directed toward those with whom you are chatting. Your brain filters out the information not relevant to where you have directed your attention. A moment later, you hear your name coming from a group of people standing nearby. Suddenly your attention is drawn elsewhere; perhaps you are trying to hear both conversations. Your brain was monitoring the other auditory material until it heard something for which you have some attention assigned, at which point the brain allowed this material to come into your awareness.

Again, my awareness is now drawn away from the click of each key as I type, confirming I have reached the target, and listening to the beeps and tones that indicate a problem with my word processing, and is now diffuse. I am now hearing the sounds of the birds outside, the television downstairs, the lawnmower in the distance, and the washing machine going through its cycle, as I have directed my attention to hear many more sounds.  It will take a few moments for my aural attention to again become directed to my typing.

It is clear that in therapy, just as much as in 'seeing' or 'hearing', our attention can be directed. If we truly believe that a solution is found in one approach, we are unlikely to see opportunities to solve the problem via another.  Our brain filters out that which we have already deemed unnecessary.

In Art Therapy, we can use the process to draw attention away from the obvious and make space for other unconscious material to present, perhaps lost in the realm of the undirected sensory data.

(If you want to understand more about directed attention, you can search for digital video media using the search phrase 'awareness test'.)

Our sensory system also operates in somewhat of a hierarchical model.  For instance, with no other sensory information, our visual system will override our auditory system. A good example of how this works is the McGurk effect.

The McGurk effect demonstrates that we can't help but integrate visual speech into what we 'hear'. If you are like most people, what you hear depends on whether your eyes are opened or closed. If your eyes are open and you are viewing the speaker's mouth, and the sound, for instance is a 'b' sound, you will probably hear a 'b'.  If however it is in contradiction to what you see, for instance, no lips coming together to push the 'b' sound out, then you will not 'hear' the 'b' sound.  No amount of awareness will cause you to hear the 'b' sound if the visual message is in contradiction to this.

For more information, search 'McGurk effect' for digital video media to see a live demonstration. Be aware, some examples are much better than others.

Clearly, our brain is more likely to believe what we see rather than what we hear, in the absence of other contradictions. This also has implications in Art Therapy. Imagine a client for whom every experience in her life has taught her she is 'not good enough'. The message may be given to her verbally, physically and in her day-to-day experiences. She may in fact perpetuate the problem by being 'not good enough'. Simply talking about a new way of being may not have enough neural engagement to effect a change. Our best practice teaching models utilise this knowledge extensively. We do not just 'talk' the lesson, we demonstrate, and finally have the student personally experience the lesson.  Of course, frequently in therapy we do the talk, but seldom in verbal therapy does the process include demonstrations or experiential work.

If we trust the senses to heal, Art Therapy can include highly powerful visual reinforcement, engage discreetly nuanced sensory systems, and allow experiential engagement that can facilitate the learning in a much more meaningful model that just words alone.

Experiential task

Gather together materials with a variety of tactile qualities. You might like to have velvet, satin, beach sand, rice, a piece of chalk, or hand cream in your collection.  Close your eyes and simply 'feel' each object for a minimum of 3 minutes each.

Without resorting to lengthy scientific explanations, feel in your body where and how this tactile experience resonates or challenges you. Does it have a 'stop' or 'go' quality?  Is it soothing or stimulating? Is it comforting or disturbing?

Consider the qualities of this sensory experience, and how you might consciously utilise this for self-care in the future.

**Further reading**

Aage R Moller, *Sensory Systems: Anatomy and Physiology*, 2002, Academic Press

Francesca Bacci and David Melcher, *Art and the Senses*, 2011, Oxford University Press

# How art heals

History demonstrates how often humans turn to art to express the most pivotal and moving events of their lives. Religious art has served as great comfort to thousands across the world and for hundreds of years. Artists have expressed their worlds, joys, tragedies and triumphs through their art works. Societies have expressed their political views and alliances through art, sculpture and performance arts for centuries. Societal changes are reflected in the building and demolishing of arts. The monuments of war, those revered and those despised tell us something about the changing cultures and societies. The statue of Saddam Hussein was constructed and erected as a celebration, and disfigured and demolished as a celebration. Humans have an innate capacity and seemingly a need to symbolize experience. We seek to find words to describe an experience in order to convey a message. It appears that we often also seek to describe through artistic means some of the most poignant experiences of our lives.

One question I am frequently asked in my role as an Art Therapist and teacher is "How does art heal?" As any Art Therapist will tell you, art making is a healing process, but our understanding about how this happens is not yet clear. Some interesting studies over the past few years demonstrate that art making is not merely a distraction technique, but that it can be a significant mood regulator.

Two studies at Boston College in the United States examined this phenomenon.

In the first study, 42 participants were exposed to material chosen to elicit a negative mood. These participants then completed one of two tasks. The first group were asked to create a drawing of anything that they liked, based upon how they were feeling at the time. The second group were instructed to copy shapes provided onto another sheet of paper. All participants were then asked to report on 'valence' (or pleasure) and 'arousal' at the end of the drawing phase. (De Petrillo & Winner, 2005) These two measures of valence and arousal are well proven measures of mood, and require a person to simply mark a point where they 'fit' on an "Affect Grid". (Russell, Weiss, & Mendelsohn, 1989)

After studying the drawings and shape copying of the participants along with their self-reported mood, it was clear that those people who drew pictures, rather than copied symbols, achieved a much happier mood. So copying symbols, or the simple task of putting pencil to paper may not be enough to generate mood change, but drawing pictures can create more positive emotion.

A second study was conducted with 75 participants to examine how mood repair occurs with art making. (Dalebroux, Goldstein, & Winner, 2008) Researchers were interested in whether the power in art making came from catharsis (expressing the negative mood) from distraction, or from positive emotional redirection. This study is particularly interesting in that it demonstrates that venting and distraction alone are not as effective as directing image making connected to a positive mood. Freud believed art making was a means of developing positive outcomes in a fantasy form, and thus creating an internal reckoning with events. The process of drawing a positive picture as a sequel to the negative image or event fits well with Freud's theory.

Most humans are motivated to achieve a 'feel good' state. We seek out methods of regulating or improving our mood. Freud called this the 'pleasure principle'. As adults, we often choose to delay gratification, and this Freud labelled the 'reality principle'. To achieve this may require a combination of cognitive and behavioural strategies that are done with full effort or concentration, in order to change a perceived uncomfortable state, either immediately, or for a delayed positive outcome. Many of the strategies people use have been previously tested by the individual and deemed an effective tool. Some people choose venting activities, some choose distraction and others choose consciously uplifting methods. Art making allows for an individualised process that can be a venting, distracting or positively focussed activity, according to the needs of the artist.

We also know that engaging in art making can reduce blood pressure, self-reported stress levels and enhance perceptions of control. It is no surprise then that many people, at many times in life, engage in art making at some level or another. Aside from professional artists, many other people doodle, sketch, photograph, collage or find some other means of expressing themselves artistically. Perhaps it is the innate physiological and mood regulating qualities of art making that draws them to such pursuits.

Art can also heal through its ability to invoke a more embodied response, to engage the sensory systems of the viewer, or to encourage empathy beyond words. Whatever it might be, the artist frequently reports a sense of success or achievement in completing the task. Many will report a sense of having been 'heard'. Some report the value for themselves in simply ordering the troubling material and externalising it.

As an Art Therapist, one of my most privileged experiences is in witnessing the journey of a client from the initial visual representations of darkness and despair, to the blossoming imagery of positive outcome, even when circumstances have not yet or cannot be changed. Creating this positive imagery frequently enhances the quality of life for the client. It is often easy to forget that anything we wish for, we must first imagine! Art Therapy enables a vivid imagining of a positive outcome and often gives great hope for the future.

The art can play many important roles. Tremendous value is found in the client's mastery of, and sense of separation from, the problem as a result of externalising the internal story. Once the client creates the image, he or she can see it outside of themselves, maintaining the problem as something not intrinsically part of them, but existing as a separate entity. This alone can ease the psychic pressure, removing shame from 'my failing' to a sense of valiant battle with the 'something' that has taken up temporary residence within him or her. Once on the page, the therapist can further enhance this by referring to the objects, images and people as marks on a page, a colour, shape or emotion separate from the client. This provides enormous safety for the client where he or she does not need to talk about or reveal details of the issue, merely his or her relationship with and manipulation of the objects on the page. A client may be more inclined to explore deeper, or to look at other ways of being, without the fear of judgement by the therapist.

Art Therapy also facilitates a window to the unconscious. In an Art Therapy client centred model, the therapist maintains the belief in the client as his or her own best healer - that he or she has the capacity within them to find new ways of being or knowing about themselves and their world. In this model, it is important to create opportunities for healing to appear from within. Although occasional psycho-education can be valuable, it is preferable that the client seeks out and finds new pathways for healing from their own resources. This model may not be the best for a therapist who is seeking repeat custom, but it is certainly the most empowering model for the individual client who will develop an awareness of their own capacity for self directed healing. Thus it is important to uncover new resources that the client possesses. Once the problem as it is known is fully expressed on the page, the Art Therapist can help make this story temporarily unknown. The therapist then assists the client to find new information from the stores of sensory material and knowledge to which the situation has not previously been directed. The unconscious can present material that may or may not be useful. This information can be interpreted by the client, tested and 'tried on' for a good fit. The new information can then be integrated into a new picture, until the insights achieved can be integrated and internalised.

Art Therapy also allows expression and nuance of sensory expression that often cannot be achieved through words alone. Many grieving parents have told me what the pain is 'like'. "I feel like I've been run over by a bus", "I feel numb", "I feel like there is a hole in my chest". None of these statements actually have any substance in reality. Most people haven't been run over by a bus to use this as a measure of pain. There is no physical numbness in grief, nor an actual hole in the chest. These expressions are approximations of the extent of sensory and emotional pain - the only words that may come close to expressing the extent of these feelings. Art Therapy can enable a person to express this pain using colour, shape, images, distance, proximity, size, depth, and symbol to name a few, along with actions such as tearing, folding, burning and cutting that add further sensory depth to the expression of the emotion. A client can feel truly heard when the art expresses a much fuller picture of the situation, including those elements for which they have few or no words to describe.

Art Therapy generally values the process as more important than the product. The art task is set not so that the final art piece has any particular magical powers, or that the art itself is the key to healing, but that the process engaged with, creates insight and potential for change. Often the art slows down the cognitive process. It may even allow sufficient time to bypass all of the usual internal dialogue about an issue, and for the mind to wander into new possibilities, dabbling here and there as time is slowed and the art keeps the focus on the issue. Asking a person to explain his or her frustration would elicit perhaps two to five minutes of probably well-rehearsed dialogue. The same talk given to perhaps a dozen friends and even a counsellor or two. Creating the art work about the frustration, not only means images can appear that hold sensory keys, but that the person has twenty minutes to roll around all of the ideas about the frustration, looking for keys and images that have probably not previously been explored. The client is dwelling with the issue. Giving it time and perhaps cognitive space not previously assigned to fully understanding the issue. As the therapist has also used mediums and tasks best suited to elicit more insight from the process, the simple engagement in perhaps a flowing manner, or a boxed process, or even in carving something away will add to the experience and process. Although a product is inevitable, it is clear here, that the process is invaluable.

There are also times when the product acts as a container for the process. There are many times in our lives when we buy reminders of experience or success. We buy souvenirs, or frame our university parchments as indicators of success. A wedding ring for instance, is much more than a piece of metal, at least for the people whose love and commitment are represented in its giving and receiving.

A handmade product for such a purpose, rich in meaning developed through the session, can be at least as important in a person's life, or even more valuable. It is imbued with the client's personal meaning. Of course, a product must only be seen as a container, and not the talisman or key to transformation itself. Products can be remade if they are lost, broken or stolen and yet the client retains the transformative journey within. Despite the risks inherent in creating products, these simple objects can often become powerful reminders of journeys taken, of resolutions made and of significant turning points. A product that sits upon the dining room table, reminding a client who has an eating disorder of the progress made in therapy can aid tremendously in the therapeutic trajectory. A book that is testimony to a difficult journey traversed and completed can also remind its creator of personal resilience. The reconnecting of a relationship may have taken many sessions and much work by the clients. A 'joined-hand' cast representing this journey may be invaluable.

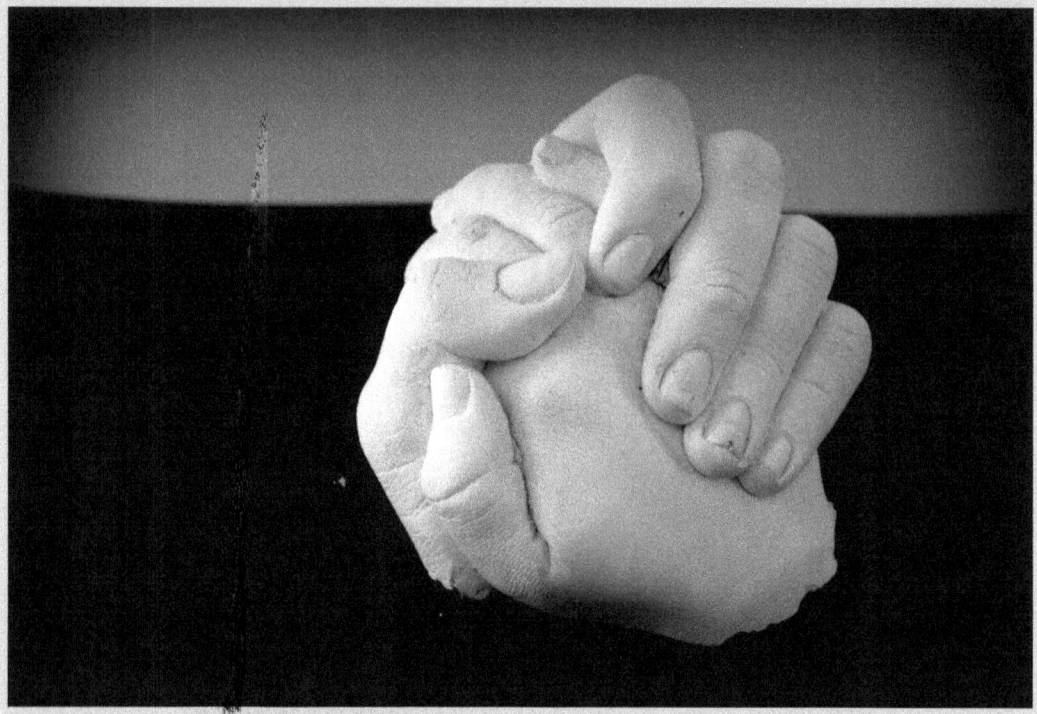

It is important not to overlook the value of words in an Art Therapy process. In many cases, an externalization of an issue onto paper can introduce new words into the standard conscious, cognitive descriptors usually used for the issue. For instance, a depressed person may regularly describe themselves as 'down', whereas the art process may reveal that the client is elevated on a great platform and is desperately alone, with a cloudiness between the client and the world below. This material can be rich with new information about the problem and its possible resolutions, leading to new verbalisations about 'loneliness' rather than 'down-ness'. The language adjustment alone may be enough to open up new awareness and possibilities for the client.

Of course, most people who come into therapy do so with a willingness to speak. They may not wish to speak about the problem that is troubling them, but in Art Therapy this is not necessary. In trusting the art to act as a third entity within the therapeutic relationship, and trusting that the client has the capacity to seek and understand paths of healing for themselves, we as the therapist, do not need to know the issue the client presents with. The therapist can use the metaphoric and symbolic language of the client to process the artwork.

# CASE STUDY ONE

| | |
|---|---|
| **Jilly:** | I came to Art Therapy because I am tired of talking about this. I don't want to tell you what it's about. I'm over it and I just want it to be better. |
| **Therapist:** | That's fine Jilly. We can work with that. What would help though is if you can identify an end point for this therapy. I will need something to work towards so I can be sure this process is useful for you. Can you tell me what it is you'd like to be better? Is it that you'd like to no longer be worried about this thing? Is it that you'd like to change a particular behaviour? |
| **Jilly:** | I want to be able to forgive someone and just get on with life. |
| **Therapist:** | So resolving the problem requires you to forgive, to let it go, and then be able to go back to your life without it taking up your energy, is this right? |
| **Jilly:** | Yes. |
| **Therapist:** | OK. Let's make a start then. If you find along the way that you have discovered a different reason for coming to these sessions make sure you let me know so we can shift the activity to help you get the most from your work here. |
| **Jilly:** | Ok |
| **Therapist:** | I am going to ask if you can represent the relationship with this unforgiven person on the page. You can just use colours and shapes, symbols, stick figures, whatever you need. Don't worry about how it looks, it is the thinking we do that matters, not any pretty art work. I'd like for something in this picture to represent yourself in this situation, and something else to show me the feelings that you have about the difficulty in forgiving. Are you able to do this for me? |
| **Jilly:** | Sure, good. |
| | (Jilly spends 12 minutes creating an image) |
| **Jilly:** | There. It's finished. |
| **Therapist:** | May I pick this up so we can look at it? |
| **Jilly:** | Yeah sure. |
| **Therapist:** | When I hold this here, does it look any different to how it looked on the table? What do you notice? |
| **Jilly:** | Hm. (Pause) I notice that I'm sort of advancing on it. (Pointing) |
| **Therapist:** | The green triangle is pushing into the orange square's space? |

| | |
|---|---|
| Jilly: | Yes. Like he's in the corner with nowhere to go. (Pause) Mmm, I guess that's true. But I don't like the grovelling. That's the pink drips. They just don't feel sincere. |
| Therapist: | So the pink drips aren't quite authentic? (Note: the therapist does not discuss 'grovelling' which would potentially lead the client into disclosure about the details when the therapist has committed that the client will not be required to do so.) |
| Jilly: | I don't suppose he has any choice really. There is no way past me. He has to grovel or be stuck there forever. But I can't forgive him when he's so insincere. (Pause) I guess I can back off without forgiving him. If I back off he might just get on with life himself, which will make it easier for me. But I can't forget what happened. I just want to put it away. These lies (pointing to an overflowing bucket) will just be with me forever. |
| Therapist: | So the bucket has a sort of permanence here that you don't like? |
| Jilly: | Yes. |
| Therapist: | Is there some other place you could put the bucket? Something you could store it in if you have to keep it? Somewhere you feel more comfortable keeping it? |
| Jilly: | Ha! I'd like to give it to him in a wheelbarrow, so he has to take it everywhere with him. He's the one who should be paying the price for what he did. (Pauses) Mmm. (looks back at therapist) |
| Therapist: | So you noticed quite a bit here and I'd like to just check in with you about what I heard you say. You told me that the green triangle has the orange square cornered, that the square has no way out, and is using the pink drips insincerely. You have suggested that perhaps the green triangle could back off, which will make things easier, as would giving the orange square a wheelbarrow carrying the bucket. Is this right? |
| Jilly: | Absolutely. It would be easier to forgive him if he was the one bearing the load. Maybe I just need to walk away and leave him with that bucket of lies, and he will have to deal with it. I can't force him to own up to this, but I guess I'll always know the truth. Actually, I think it would be good for me to forgive him, but actually I think it is just being able to walk away and accept that no matter how much I fight the battle and corner him, I can't make him own up to stuff, and this just means that I have to be constantly exposed to that grovelling. Maybe all I really want to be able to do is to walk away. |
| Therapist: | So green triangle being able to walk away here is the key. |
| Jilly: | Yes. Yes absolutely. |
| Therapist: | I am wondering if you can use scissors and tape, and a new sheet of paper to remake the story how you'd like it to be? |
| Jilly: | (After some thought) Yes. I can. I'd like to keep him in the corner, but boxed in by his own lies. Yes, in a wheelbarrow. I don't know if I can draw a wheelbarrow! And |

I'd like to put me way over here, with my back to him. That way, he can walk away, but he'll have to take the barrow, and I won't see whether he does it or not, and I don't care. It's his mess and even if he doesn't own up to it now, he knows what he's responsible for. By me not listening anymore, his grovelling will be useless.

**Therapist:** Let's do it shall we?

**Jilly:** (after the reconstruction of the drawing) Wow. I wonder why I didn't get this before? I think I thought that forgiving him would somehow get rid of the lies and be the key to me moving on, but actually it's just about me moving away. I don't have to forgive him until he shows the appropriate amount of remorse instead of his grovelling excuses. Even if he never does that, I can still have a life and be happy. I don't have to lay awake every night making up conversations to convince him to confess. It's just a waste of energy. I LIKE this picture! Thank you.

As the therapist, one might be battling curiosity in these situations. What did he do to her? Will she be carrying a seed of anger and resentment because she hasn't forgiven him? Is she walking away from an important relationship? These are all valid questions but in a client centred approach; we support the client to explore possibility and to achieve a goal. If my client's goal is to feel comfortable wearing tea cosies on her head in the middle of summer, so be it. Provided this action brings no harm to herself or others, I will support her in her efforts. She may well decide that this action causes her social pain, and again the choice will be hers, does she want assistance to let go of her tea cosy wearing habit, or does she want to let go of society's expectations of her? In working with a client where the details of the situation have not been revealed, it is extremely important to trust the art process, and trust the client's capacity to guide and heal their own lives.

Art heals in ways we are yet to fully understand. What is clear is that an engagement with a sensory, symbolic medium adds something that cannot quite be captured in usual verbal counselling models. Of course, for many, Art Therapy will not be the desired medium through which they would seek psychological support and healing. But for those who are willing and those for whom verbal therapy has not provided an avenue for healing, art may well be a wonderful and effective alternative.

Experiential task

Consider a small issue regarding which you would like some insight.
Using a moveable medium, such as a soft pastel, create a symbolic representation of this
situation.  Be sure to add plenty of detail, and include yourself in the image.
Put the image up where you will see it easily over the next few days.

Each time you stop to look at the image ask yourself "What can the art tell me about itself?"
Imagine the art answering back with statements beginning with "I am..." or "I feel..."

**Further Reading**

Shaun McNiff, *Art Heals: How Creativity Cures the Soul*, 2004, Shambhala

Pat Allen, *Art Is a Way of Knowing*, 1995, Shambhala

# Creating the therapeutic environment

The appropriate environment for Art Therapy clearly varies significantly to that of a verbal counselling space. The requirements for physical comfort, safety, guarantee of confidentiality, and neutrality are essentially the same. However equipment and the nature of the work mean some compromises must be made. A table is essential in order to spread materials out and create ease for the art making. It is useful to have this table easily moved to the side, or to have an additional space within the same room to explore other ways of working, such as empty chair work, psychodrama, body work. Materials need to be easily accessible and a variety of art and craft making equipment gives flexibility to the therapy. This equipment is best kept in a neat and orderly fashion so as to not overwhelm the client's sensory system. Likewise, colour is a wonderful thing, but be aware of colour's capacity to influence behaviour.

It may seem wise to create a calming, nurturing space, but if you are working with a client who is seeking to develop assertiveness, (e.g. a submissive woman who is a victim of domestic abuse) or a shy child, perhaps 'calm' is not what you want your client to feel. Energised might be better! Music needs a similar caution. Music can be truly wonderful in therapy, but it must be used thoughtfully, not just as a default option. Music can so influence mood, and mood profoundly influences engagement. Perhaps you have panpipes gently playing in the background, when the title soundtrack from "Chariots of Fire" (Hudson, 1981) might be needed!

Some Art Therapists will be fortunate enough to have a facility well suited to Art Therapy, which includes easels and stools. For Art Therapists who work in a variety of settings, or even in a client's home, it is important to carefully consider the therapeutic environment, and especially the workspace seating. Seating is best arranged so that the therapist is at 90 degrees to the client. This enables the therapist to view the artwork in almost the same perspective as the client. It allows the therapist to see the client clearly (directly alongside makes viewing his or her facial expressions difficult). This positioning does not place a large table top between the client and therapist as it would if the therapist sat on one side and the client on the other. Placing the client along the non-dominant side of the therapist allows the therapist to take notes without placing them in the space between the client and themselves. From this position it is also possible to assist the client in art making - holding something down for sticking, sharpening a broken pencil and so on. It also allows for those moments when a touch of the client's hand or shoulder is useful.

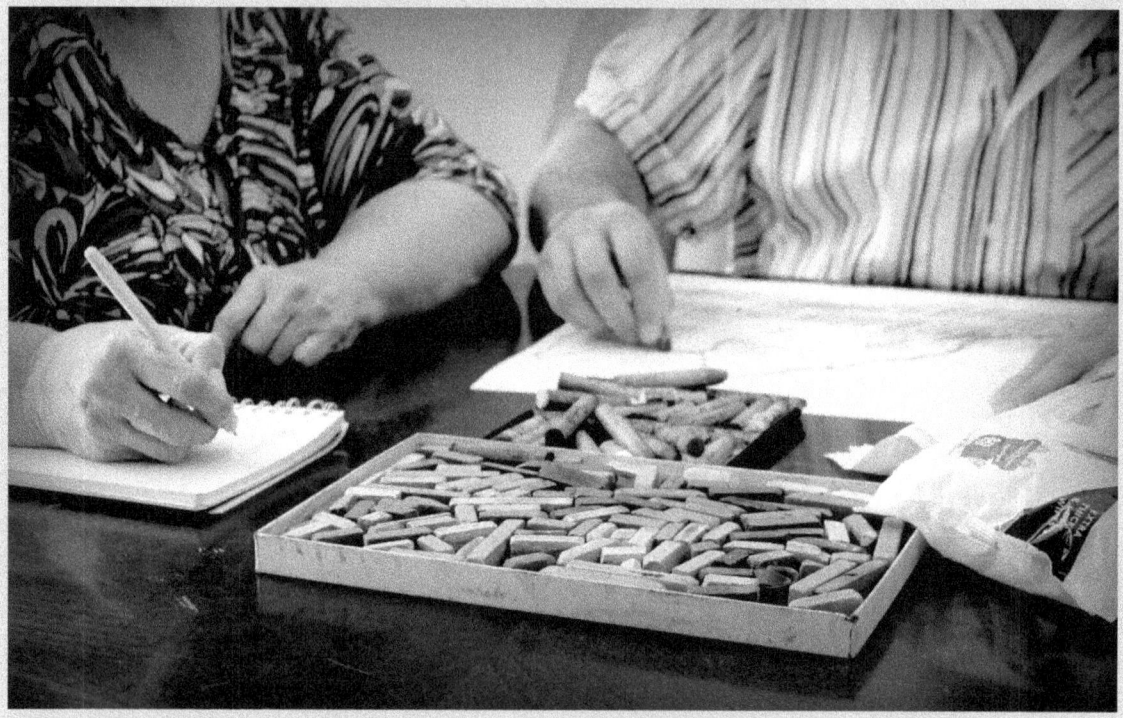

*The therapist sits alongside the client, ensuring the note taking does not form a barrier between themselves and the client.*

Whilst many new therapists find note taking difficult, it is an important skill to acquire and an essential element of good therapy. It is surprisingly difficult to remember after more than a couple of minutes the exact words a client may use, or the metaphor they so vividly expressed that will be immensely beneficial in reflecting back to the client when the art work or the session is complete. When the therapist asks the client to create an image, it is wise to note this also in case the client asks for the question or task to be repeated. Even subtle changes in this repeated request can interrupt the process for the client. Always consider note taking when you are setting up the therapeutic space.

The considerations for therapeutic space should not end with the physical requirements, but must extend to the physical, spiritual and intellectual preparation of the therapist. A therapist who rushes in from battling traffic and dropping children at basketball needs at least 10 minutes to focus energies before welcoming the first client. Previous case notes need to be perused and most recent notes read fully. Equipment needs to be ready, and the therapist needs to have re-centred and perhaps engaged in some useful ritual or meditation to be spiritually prepared to provide safe, judgement-free containment and support for his or her client. The therapist needs to have sufficient self-awareness, and psychological support (probably in the form of clinical supervision) of his or her own to be able to provide Unconditional Positive Regard (Rogers, 1951) for the client.

Experiential task

Practice making notes while watching a documentary, or ask a friend to talk to you for some time while you make notes of the conversation. Note taking can be almost invisible in the session and can serve both the therapist and the client. The only way to be a good note taker is to practice, practice, practice. Begin before you start to work with clients.

**Further Reading**

Michael Kahn, *Between Therapist and Client: The New Relationship*,

Revised edition, 1997, Holt Paperbacks

## PART TWO   The Act of Therapy

## A simple one-to-one model

When a client presents for Art Therapy, they have usually attended of their own volition, either with an understanding of Art Therapy, or at the very least with an expectation that art will be involved in some way.  A client will also come with something to work on.  They may not yet have determined exactly what this is, but very few people, if indeed any, will pay for an Art Therapy session without some intention for doing so.  The client then has a 'goal' for therapy.

Mandated clients surprisingly also come with a goal. It may be that they seek to fulfil the requirements of the order. It may be that they wish to "get this over and done with", or that they "want people to get off my back". Each of these is a goal just as valid for the therapeutic starting point, as is a goal specifically about self-improvement.

In a client centred model, the client's goal becomes the therapist's goal, provided it fits within moral, ethical and professional guidelines. It is important that this goal, once uncovered, be refined and documented by the therapist.

In the first instance the therapist may ask the client to create an artwork, images, symbols colours and shapes that best represents the 'problem' as it is.  This artwork may be simple or elaborate, literal or symbolic, but ideally will include the client somewhere in the image.

Whilst the client creates, the therapist sits quietly observing and making notes.  Many new therapists find this a difficult task, and feel as if they should be doing something whilst his or her client works, in order to remove the focus and thus diminish anxiety about art making.  This may serve this purpose in the short term, but once a client has begun the process he or she will quickly become accustomed to the Art Therapist's presence. Following this, the client will feel greater support and the therapeutic alliance will strengthen if the therapist traverses the journey literally alongside the client.

It is important for the therapist to be fully observant of the client during the process, monitoring the art making, facial expressions, body language, challenges in the task, hesitations and libidinal energy shifts. These cues can be invaluable in the reflection process.

Note taking is another task many new therapists feel interferes in the therapeutic alliance, believing that whilst note taking the therapist fails to attend fully to the client. In fact, the opposite is to some extent true. Although never lifting your eyes from the note book would indeed be not attending to your client, brief note taking often validates the client's experience. He or she can feel 'heard' and that the words spoken are valuable and important. If a client is aware that he or she can access these notes at any time, then there is seldom concern about what the therapist writes and more of a sense of validation and the professionalism of the therapist.

Note taking is important during the session, as observing actions and choices and hearing or seeing the metaphors the client uses can easily be forgotten. Yet it is these non-verbal, and non-linear cues that provide access to unconscious material. Note taking is a habit that can be developed with subtleness in the action that still keeps the client at the centre of the therapist's attention.

Attending to notes, also gives the therapist a wonderful opportunity to not attend to notes. Momentarily putting them aside can create an increased intimacy and place greater import on the therapeutic material immediately at hand.

Once the initial artwork is complete, the therapist begins the discussion. In verbal therapies most questions asked by the therapist are open ended. Asking open-ended questions encourages the client to make meaning of what she or he has observed and then to reduce this to words in order to convey this to the therapist. In verbal therapy, this is the wisest and most appropriate choice. In Art Therapy, it is likely that many questions will be closed ended, encouraging the client to use a yes/no approach to further define and highlight areas of concern, interest or resolution in the art work. In Art Therapy the aim is for the client to make the known, unknown, to suspend normal conscious cognitive thought and allow sensory and preverbal intelligences to guide the therapy. Ideally, the client can stay in the 'unworded', and more sensory space, for as long as possibly, manipulating the art for insight. At some point, usually toward the end of a session, the client may well create a worded explanation for the insights gained and at this point a fully cognitive and verbal summarisation can be quite appropriate in reinforcing the insights or learning.

In further unpacking the process that follows the art making, it is important to understand three important parallel concepts:

## Phenomenology

Though there are many definitions and theories regarding the true nature of phenomenology, the easiest system is one where phenomenology is seen as a sort of anti-philosophy. In philosophy, the nature of something is explored as a supposed absolute truth, separate to any human experience of the 'thing'. It is seeking 'true matter'. If you think about a chair for instance, a philosopher will examine the parts, the purpose, the societal constructs, the assumptions and so on until the chair is completely 'known'. In a phenomenological exploration, the chair will be considered, first and foremost, NOT a chair. How the chair intersects with human experience, and each individual's human experience at that, is the key to a phenomenological exploration. A chair is only known as a chair because of a human capacity and desire to sit, because people have used a chair for centuries for such a purpose, and because our language has deemed it so. Despite this, humans can sit in many positions and on many surfaces. A chair would not be so, if it weren't for a sitter. Thus any non-sitter viewing the chair for the first time would have no concept of such a device. The chair does not carry meaning separate from the meaning assigned it by the viewer. Of course, a pure phenomenological approach is not possible. It is impossible to remove all constructions and impositions - cultural, religious or aesthetic, common sense or even scientific - from our perception of the object or experience. Yet this is the task we attempt, if the primary rule of phenomenology is to first understand something from within.

In Art Therapy a client is first asked to not make any presuppositions as to the meaning or content of what he or she sees, but to merely see the colours and shapes on the page. We ask the client to have an internal experience of the view. Reducing it to words is not necessary, but just to see, feel, and draw it in upon one's senses.

## Heuristics

Heuristics are trial and error, experience-based techniques for problem solving, learning, and discovery. It is a procedure that enables a reduction to the most likely or relevant answer. In the second stage of the process, the Art Therapist asks the client "does this fit with your experience?" The client 'tests' the hypothesis, and then rejects or accepts it, modifying the process along the way. For instance, the client may respond, "Actually, yes, it is like my experience, but not all the time, only on weekends". By a process of elimination and/or matching, possible resolutions are identified.

## Hermeneutics

Hermeneutics, in its modern use of the term, refers to the interpretation of texts, or other media, in particular in light of meanings constructed from the position of an individual within a social context. The earliest reference to hermeneutics is in relation to the interpretation of biblical texts. These scholars asked, "How can we understand these lessons in the context of our current social environment and how can we understand these texts independent of social construct? What does it mean?"

The hermeneutic approach holds that the most basic fact of social life is the meaning of an action. Social life is constituted by social actions, and actions are meaningful to the actors and to the other social participants. Moreover, subsequent actions are oriented towards the meanings of prior actions; so understanding the later action requires that we have an interpretation of the meanings that various participants assign to their own actions and those of others. (Little, 2008)

A hermeneutic process within Art Therapy seeks to have the client find meaning for his or her responses and beliefs about the artwork and the representation of experience expressed within it. We ask the client, "What might this mean to and for you? How does this have meaning for you as a member of society, and how does this have meaning for you as an individual, without the constraints of social expectation?"

A phenomenological, heuristic and hermeneutic process, attempts to 'see' fully, to test hypothesis for solutions, learning or discovery, to interpret what is seen, and to discover meanings for such notions, dependant and independent of social construct. It is observing one's lived experience, making a discovery and then understanding it.

It sounds very complex yet can occur quite gently, and within a short time.

The following demonstrates these concepts in action.

# CASE STUDY TWO

**Client GOAL:** *To find ways of moving on after a relationship breakdown.*

**Therapist:** Can you draw for me something that represents the situation as it is now? What it feels like? Where you are in this story? Just let the ideas come and don't argue with them, let them be on the paper. Take as long as you need. Let your heart and body guide your mind in creating this.

(The art is created)

**Therapist:** Does this look like the situation as it is now? (Holding the art work parallel to the client's face and at about 60 - 80cms distance)

**Client:** (Pausing) Yes. I think so. It is very dark though.

**Therapist:** It's dark? Is this the darkness you want to depict or does it need adjusting?

**Client:** No. It's fine. I just feel quite confronted by it that's all.

**Therapist:** So the darkness in the art is confronting?

**Client:** Uh huh... that's when it began, (pointing to a stick figure), when I broke up with Justin, and it just stretches all the way across (pointing to the dark area)

**Therapist:** So the darkness begins with the blue figure and stretches across? Is this across time or something else?

**Client:** Yes. But, (pausing and thinking), I guess really it's also that after the breakup with Justin it stretched into nearly every corner of my life. It sort of overwhelmed me really.

**Therapist:** So the darkness stretched out from this blue figure, and it has stretched into this timeline (pointing to the length of the darkness) and it has stretched into most areas on the page?

**Client:** Yup, absolutely.

**Therapist:** Do you notice anything about the art work when you look at it now? Perhaps something that jumps out at you, or that you didn't notice before?

**Client:** (Thinking) mmm... I didn't give Justin a face, only a boofy head.

**Therapist:** Do you want the blue figure to have a face?

**Client:** Hell no. I never want to see that face again.

**Therapist:** So the blue figure is best without a face here?

**Client:** That's right.

| | |
|---|---|
| Therapist: | (Still holding the art work), Anything else? |
| Client: | No, I don't think so. |
| Therapist: | If you were to give this image a one-word title, what would it be? |
| Client: | "Shite" |
| Therapist: | "Shite". Ok. (Jotting this in the notes) We will have another look at it this way again soon. I am going to ask you to do something a little strange here. I am going to turn your artwork on its side. What I am hoping is that you can look at it with fresh eyes. Try not to think about it as you intended it to be, but just see whatever jumps out at you. Ok? |
| Client: | Sure |
| Client: | (Pausing) Mmmm, this is ridiculous but it looks like a bat hanging in a cave, just before it takes off you know, with its wings stretched out? |
| Therapist: | Ahh ok. I can see that. |
| Client: | Is this what you wanted me to do? |
| Therapist: | Oh yes, it's great. |
| Client: | It looks like I'm climbing up some sheer cliff here. But I was being blown away and falling over when we looked at it before. |
| Therapist: | So with bat wings stretched out, and the green figure climbing up a sheer cliff, how does it feel for you? |
| Client: | Well, I'd far rather be climbing a sheer cliff, because that's courageous, than just being blown over. And the bat, well I don't know, maybe I'm about to wake up and fly out of the dark cave? |
| Therapist: | And the feeling? |
| Client: | Well, I guess courageous, and umm, hopeful. |
| Therapist: | Does this fit with what you believe about the situation? Does it require courage and hope? |
| Client: | I guess so, a bit yeah, because I've come here haven't I? I'm ready to fly out of that awful place. But I don't know how yet. I guess I haven't worked out how to use my wings. |
| Therapist: | This might be a good thing to come back to later, this "how to use my wings". What do you think? |
| Client: | Yes. That'd be good. |
| Therapist: | Is there anything else you notice on this page? |

| | |
|---|---|
| **Client:** | No. |
| **Therapist:** | Does this image have a different name now? |
| **Client:** | Yes, it's definitely different. Ummm... " Mountaineering" |
| **Therapist:** | Let's turn it again, so the image is upside down. Remember what we did last time? Just try to see this image with fresh eyes. Be open to whatever stands out for you. (Therapist turns the artwork) |
| **Client:** | Ha! Jason looks like an onion in the ground! (Laughing) |
| **Therapist:** | The blue figure is now an onion? |
| **Client:** | Yes! It brings tears to my eyes. |
| **Therapist:** | Happy tears? Sad tears? |
| **Client:** | (Serious now)    I'm not sure yet. I guess they have been sad tears for so long, but they might be different now. |
| **Therapist:** | So you're not sure yet. That's ok. We'll go on. Do you see anything else this way? |
| **Client:** | It seems lighter somehow, like it's about to take off.  Nothing else though. |
| **Therapist:** | And does this orientation have a title? |
| **Client:** | Yes, "freedom" |
| **Therapist:** | Ok. Freedom. Let's look at it in the last odd angle.  What do you see? |
| **Client:** | Oh. I don't like that, it's awful. It's like I'm falling into a fiery hell, and Justin is standing at the top laughing at me.  No, that's terrible. |
| **Therapist:** | Shall we turn it back to the original position? |
| **Client:** | No, I need to do a title first, don't I? |
| **Therapist:** | Sure, if you are fine to keep it in this position for a bit longer. |
| **Client:** | Yes, yes I am.  Wow, this is like giving up.  Yes the title is "Painful Surrender".  Oops, that's two words is that ok? |
| **Therapist:** | That's fine.  "Painful Surrender" it is, in this orientation.  Are you ready for us to turn it? |
| **Client:** | Yes! Please do. |
| **Therapist:** | So now we are back to your original picture.  Does it look any different to you now? |
| **Client:** | (After a generous pause) yes actually, it feels more like I am running than being pushed away and falling over.  Also Justin looks sad. |

| | |
|---|---|
| **Therapist:** | To begin this artwork, I asked if you could create the image of your life as it is now, with the painful breakup still impacting on your life. Is this image still accurate for that do you think? |
| **Client:** | Mmmm. I guess it is but, you know, I actually think Justin doesn't need to be in the picture. I mean he's not now. He's gone, moved on, life's rosy for him. Maybe I just need to cut him out of my life, and my thinking now. |
| **Therapist:** | Would you actually like to do this? Cut him out? |
| **Client:** | Off the end? (Indicating with her fingers how she'd like to 'cut him off' the page) Mmm. Yes. |
| **Therapist:** | Let's make it a nice clean cut to begin with in case you feel you want to reattach the blue figure to the scene. |
| **Client:** | (cuts off the blue figure, tests its belonging by putting it back and taking it away). No. I like it gone. |
| **Therapist:** | What would you like to do with the blue figure now? |
| **Client:** | Part of me wants to set fire to him and burn it, but I think the better part of me wants to put him in the garden. I guess I do want him to be happy, as long as I can be happy too. |
| **Therapist:** | Let's look at the image again, and rotate it. (Lifting art work back in parallel to the client's face) |
| **Client:** | Whoa! It feels really different somehow. Like all the weightiness is gone. I guess when I think about it, I've always wanted Justin to still be in the story, to still be looking on and seeing me suffering, just to prove how much I loved him and how much it hurts me. But really, doing that just has me still making decisions about things according to how it will affect him, not about how it will affect me. |

Despite the simplicity here, (and the unlikely, quickly gained insights), it is surprising how often this approach does work, and for this reason, this basic method is probably the simplest and most effective technique to begin the Art Therapy process.

Of course, even without such quick insight, the early dialogue provides enough material for extensive further exploration. The therapist might begin with the faceless blue figure, or the bat wings in readiness for flight. The other figure climbing up a sheer cliff may lead to strengths recognition; the onion and tears, freedom, courage, and surrender as the Hero's Journey, (Campbell, 1949) The sadness of the blue figure, the desire for it to be in a garden, or indeed in another parallel universe, the desire to 'burn' this figure are also paths for exploration.

Experiential task

Draw a representation of a situation that you currently find a little confusing.
Stand back from the image and describe what you see, what you notice now that you didn't notice before, what you see in the image that you didn't intend, and what you notice about the spaces in the image.

Rotate the image and spend at least three minutes truly 'looking' at what you see, not just what you intended to see when you drew the picture.

Consider how this action has facilitated insight for you.

**Further Reading**

Mala Gitlin Betensky, *What Do You See?: Phenomenology of Therapeutic Art Expression*, 1995, Jessica Kingsley

The Archive for Research in Archetypal Symbolism, *The Book Of Symbols: Reflections On Archetypal Images*, 2010, Tachen

Cathy Malchiodi, *Art Therapy Sourcebook*, 2006, McGraw-Hill

# Mediums

The one tool Art Therapists have, that verbal counsellors frequently do not, is the art. It is easy to recognise the power of the art to effect insight and transformation. Yet the use of the art tool, and in particular the qualities of the medium, is often neglected. Understanding, observing and utilising the qualities of the medium can greatly enhance the therapeutic outcome.

In Expressive Therapies Continuum, Hinz, (2009) discusses the qualities of mediums as an important consideration in serving the therapeutic goal. Every medium and action engaged in the Art Therapy process can be examined and tailored to best serve the client's goal.

**Consider the size:**

Is the client best supported if the art to be created is large or small? Does the client need the art to grow what is being depicted, or does it need to be contained? A representation of current anxiety may best be represented on a small page if the therapeutic goal is served when the issue is small. Or perhaps the client has the necessary resources to see the 'non-sense' of the issue when it is created comically large?

**Consider the bodily engagement with the size:**

Does the client become aggressive and demonstrative when the anxiety is large? Depicting the 'large' anxiety, where the bodily movements required to make such an image would also be large, and somewhat uncontained, may be counterproductive.

Perhaps the client has a small, simmering but well contained anxiety. The large page coercing his or her body to open out physically to create such an image may provide quite a release.

**Consider the physical engagement with the medium:**

Does this medium require gentle handling, for example tissue paper, just as the issue needs a gentle approach? Does the medium require great effort to shape, for instance, carving, just as learning to live with challenging circumstances might need time, patience and great effort to master? Does the medium lend itself to grand gestures, resonating with great sweeping changes in the client's life?

**Consider the medium itself:**

If the anxiety is due to uncontrollable elements in the client's life, choosing a less controllable medium will resonate with this sense of helplessness. Marbling is a highly uncontrollable medium, and can be used to resonate with a family's sense of helplessness when a child is dying. No matter how hard the artist tries, the medium, will go its own way, much like the disease ravaging their child's body.

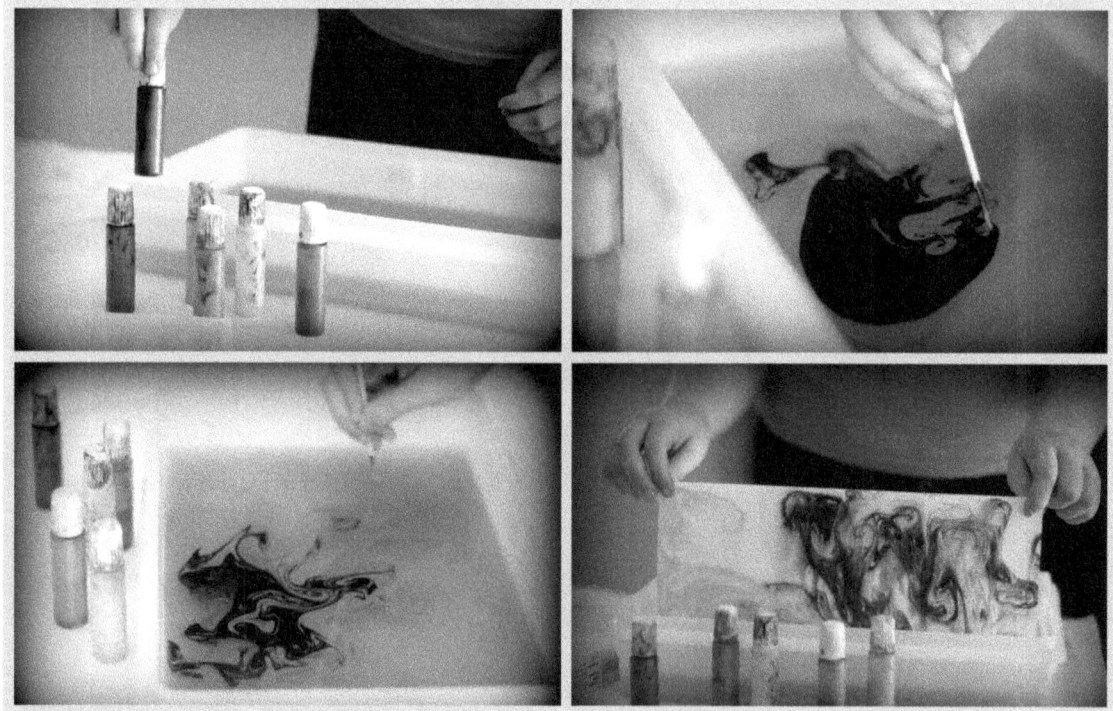

*The Marbling Process*

A 16 year old, with end stage Cystic Fibrosis, on being asked to create some heart designs. "It's a bit like life really, no matter how hard you try, it just goes its own way. But it's still pretty. I guess there is still some beautiful things about my life, it's just not the way I'd do it, if I had a choice."

Imagine offering marbling to a client whose anxiety is caused through always being inflexible, controlled and controlling. Ask them to make a star in the design, and within a few minutes this client will be highly challenged by the medium. Will this assist the client in achieving the therapeutic goal? A person seeking great control of their environment and the people around them, may find the flowing medium extremely challenging, which may, or may not be desirable and so must be considered within the context of the therapeutic goal.

If anxiety is due to a frustration because of a lack of freedom, a soft, uncontrollable medium may offer the freedom required. Perhaps soft chalk pastels will add to the process. Using markers gives great permanence to what is committed to paper and may suit a client with great resolve. Perhaps the act of making a paper pulp and reforming it into something new may hold qualities of the action required in the client's life.

Carefully considering the medium provides yet another opportunity for therapeutic impact upon the senses and in effecting change.

Experiential task

Explore many mediums. Ask yourself, what are the qualities in relation to size in the art making? What are the qualities of the medium? What are the qualities of engaging with the medium? With what experiences might each of these qualities cause resonance or challenge?

**Further Reading**

Lisa Hinz, *Expressive Therapies Continuum: A Framework for Using Art in Therapy*, 2009, Routledge

Judith Aron Rubin, (Ed), *Approaches to Art Therapy: Theory and Technique*, 2001, Routledge

## Broadening the model

In order to further explore the art, the therapist may use one of many techniques. The possibilities are endless and only limited by the therapist's knowledge and experience with art making, mediums and qualities. It is for this reason that ongoing personal art making is so important for students, and indeed for experienced Art Therapists. It is essential to be practiced and confident to move fluently from one art process to another and to be quite sure of how the medium will respond to, and assist, the client in achieving outcomes consistent with the goal. Training also gives the student an ear for the sensory and experiential metaphors that a client uses to dialogue with the art, and this provides cues for the therapist in offering further direction.

Experiential task

Take a piece of art created in an earlier session. When you consider the art, what would you like to do with it that has some resonance with your understanding of the situation now? Respond accordingly.

What does this 'act' add into the cognitive processing of the issue?

### Further Reading

Susan I Buchalter, *Art Therapy Techniques and Applications: A Model for Practice*, 2009, Jessica Kingsley Publishers

Catherine Moon, *Materials & Media in Art Therapy: Critical Understandings of Diverse Artistic Vocabularies*, 2010, Routledge

# Extent and Amelioration

A very important and simple art task is an extent and amelioration exercise. The aim is for this quick activity to provide a measure of the extent of the problem, and at a later date to ascertain if any amelioration has occurred. The client is asked to draw a simple shape that best represents the size, shape and colour of the issue, and with the space on the page taken up, representing the space this issue takes up in the client's life. This is a much richer picture than the "On a scale of 1 – 10, how much of a problem is this to you now?"

Clients may not have words to describe the subtle changes that occur, but may well make the colour a little lighter, or the angles a little less sharp in subsequent assessments. These art works are best kept by the therapist, and each time a new assessment is done, the client needs to have previous assessments to view prior to completing the current measure.

This activity alone can be very powerful in acknowledging and celebrating successes, however small, especially in slow and difficult journeys. It is also a wonderful art process to use in ending rituals once the therapy is complete, and for a celebratory reflection upon the journey.

*An Extent and Amelioration exercise*

Experiential task

Think about a current situation that is proving a little troubling but that you know will be resolved.  Create an 'extent' image. How big is the problem? How much space does it take up on the page? What colour and shape is it?

Note in your calendar or diary to come back to this in three weeks and complete the 'amelioration' exercise. How big is the problem now? How much space does it take up on the page? What colour and shape is it?

Try not to reduce this to intellect or words, just depict the sensory experience of the circumstance; how it feels.

**Further Reading**

Gerald D. Oster and Patricia Gould Crone, *Using Drawings in Assessment and Therapy: A Guide for Mental Health Professionals*, 2004, Routledge

# Cutting: doors, windows and peepholes

In the Case Study Two, the client stated "Maybe I just need to cut him out of my life..." The therapist immediately responded to this by seeing how the worded metaphor could be enacted in the artwork. The therapist also directed the client to make it a 'clean cut' as she is familiar with the material's propensity to not reattach cleanly should the client find the detachment confronting.

The client's words will very frequently direct the process. The comment, "I do/don't know what's behind this", can lead to an exploratory window in the artwork, in order to create what is behind. A client may state that she 'just wants to put her troubles aside'. If the artwork lends itself to removing just the 'troubles', then it is quite feasible to do so, and to explore the implications of doing so in her day-to-day life.

"The Obediant Daughter"

Out of the frame my parents put me in.

original page with frame removed, glued to a larger sheet.

Paper glued over with new message.

"Following my own dreams."

*Frame removal by cutting, and further adaption of the image*

Experiential task

Using an art piece constructed in a previous session, look for opportunities to cut something off, to cut a peephole into 'what is behind' or to cut a doorway or flap to 'open up' and explore, and then to symbolically close.

Place another piece of paper underneath the original and draw what you see through the peephole or behind the door.

How does this act extend your understanding of the situation?

# Folding

Each action leads to a new art piece and a new opportunity for exploration. "If I could just close the distance between us" may lead to a folding of the page to bring the elements together.

For example, folding the page may conceal other items on the page that the client may deem too important to ignore, and thus the page is unfolded again and a new shift in awareness occurs.

Experiential task

Consider a situation where you sometimes wish you could move something out of the way, or ignore it for a time. Hold the folding idea in mind whilst you create an image that symbolically represents this situation. As a therapist you would not ask a client to consider the capacity for folding the image before creating it, but often in session you will notice the capacity and potential for the folding to be a therapeutic act, once the image is viewed.

Use a folding technique to try out the situation with or without the element you would like to remove or ignore.

Pay careful attention to the feelings that result when you reveal and hide. How might this serve your client?

"She is always getting between us.
I can't forget she was his first wife.
Gave birth to his kids.
We don't have that Glue."

Art Piece before the fold

"Wow, we even get to share the same cloud."
"I don't need to get rid of her, just fold her into the background."
(and white-out that extra kiss!")

Art Piece following the fold

# Magnifying

A very useful and effective technique is a magnifying process. The therapist may discuss with the client how a magnifier is used in order to see greater detail in something. The client is then asked to observe a small area identified as potentially valuable for further examination, as if it is under a microscope, or magnifying glass, and to recreate this part of the image in larger form with greater detail on a new page. An A4 size page with a simple line drawing of a magnifying glass, and the centre removed can be particularly helpful. It is best to leave the surrounding page intact in order to mask some of the image underneath and allow the focus to be drawn directly to the area revealed in the smaller circle.

While moving this faux magnifying glass across the image, the client is supported to consider the finer details in this part of the story, and to include feelings, thoughts, facts and elements that add to the overall understanding of the situation. It is important to explain that magnifying an image usually gives us greater detail we could not see before, so the client is instructed to just trust what comes up and to include it in this magnified image. Again, this resulting image may be rotated to make the known unknown. Moving away from the image and viewing it from a greater distance can also create opportunity to make the known image, somewhat unknown, allowing for further insight.

Please do not use a real magnifying glass for this process, or the client will simply redraw the original picture larger, with probably very little added detail.

Experiential task

Consider a person that you feel you might not understand well. Create a symbolic representation of your current perception of that person.
Make a 'magnifying glass' with a lens size of approximately 5cms and place this page over the image. Move it around until an area appears that you can further explore for more understanding of the person chosen for this task.

Recreate this 'window' on another large piece of paper, taking up as much space as possible, but within a circular shape. Just allow possibilities to present in the art.

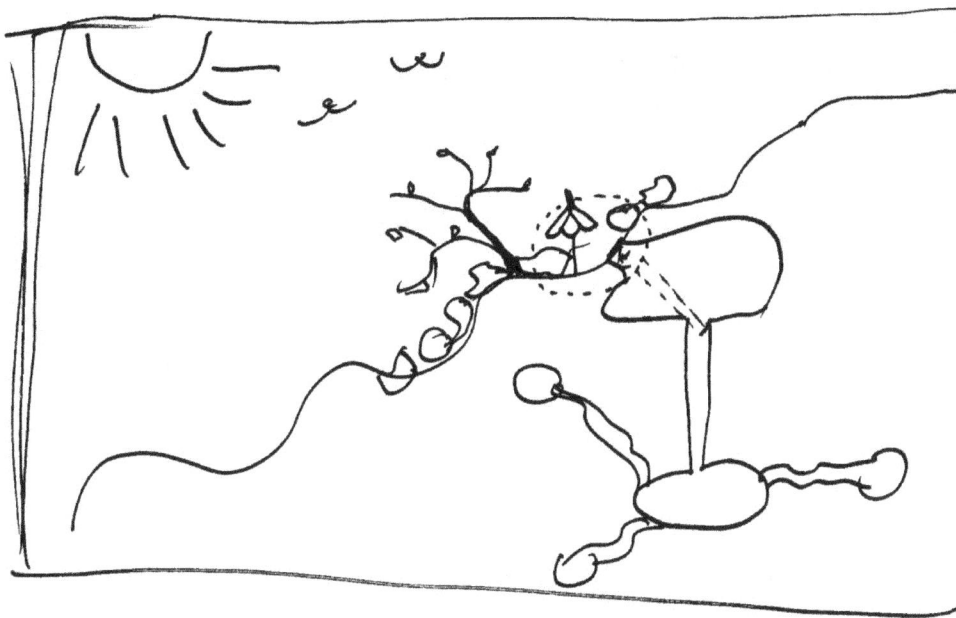

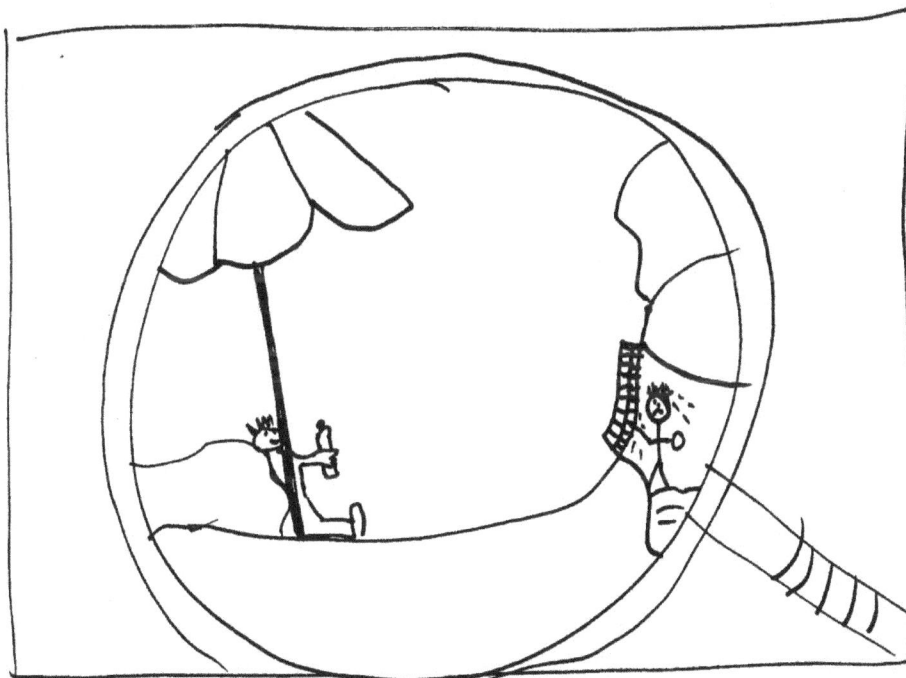

"I thought it was just one thing stopping me, but actually, it's lots. lots of small barriers"

*Magnifying the image*

# Before and after scenes

A client may also benefit from creating the scene that occurs prior to the one depicted in the first process, or even the scene that follows.  This technique can form the entire therapeutic approach if desired, with a client creating a 'start point' and an 'end point' in terms of the goal, and each art work between a stepped approach to achieving the goal. This is best used when the trajectory for the goal is quite straightforward, and is a less useful technique in exploring a range of possibilities.

Experiential task

Consider a time where you made what you now recognise as a poor decision.  Create the moment of the 'poor decision' image.  For the next art piece, depict the consequences of this poor decision, or the after picture. Next consider the events that led to this poor decision. Create an image to represent the before picture.  Put the three images together and process according to the method described earlier in this text. What do you see?

Finally, create a wish picture. If you could have done things differently, have would you wish things could have turned out?

Note how each of these processes assist in understanding and self-forgiveness.

*Creating before and after scenes*

*Creating a 'wish picture'*

## Confusion and Clarity

Where confusion is the primary issue at hand a client may benefit from completing a 'confusion' image first, depicting the elements of the situation in no particular order. After the basic processing of the art work, the client is asked to create another art work entitled 'clarity', where the task is to utilise unconscious wisdom to simply order and rearrange the initial image on a new page, adding or removing elements that can practically be added or removed in the situation, to create an image that has feelings of clarity.

The processing of this second art work can frequently elicit valuable details, although it is important to pre-warn the client that this is a starting point and will not 'magically' provide answers, but will perhaps point to some.

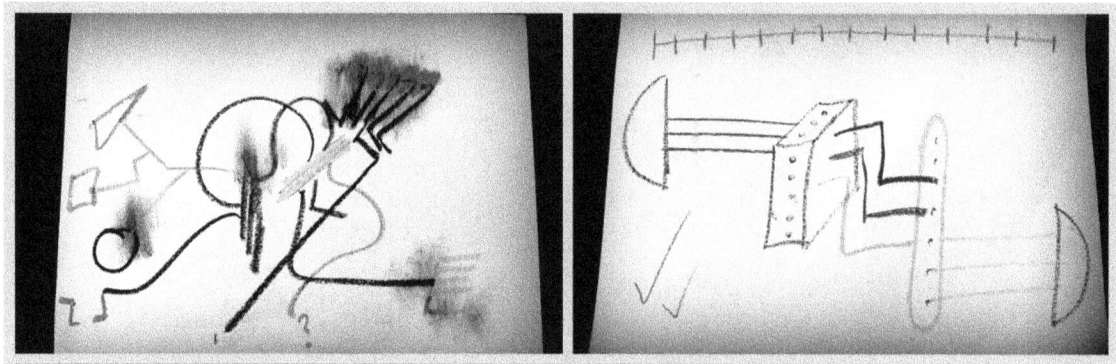

*Confusion*                                      *Clarity*

Experiential task

Consider a situation that is currently puzzling you.
Create the 'confusion' image, process this, and then move onto creating the 'clarity' image.

## Question and resolution

Adapting the previous model slightly, the client can create 'question' and 'answer' artworks. It is not the 'resolution' itself that the client creates but the resulting circumstance or situation if this 'question' is resolved. The formal processing of the art works is essential in accessing the client's unconscious store of resources for a suitable answer. Again, this process may lead to valuable information but is unlikely to magically provide a clear answer itself. Many clients will report a significant shift in thinking in the days that follow this exercise.

Experiential task

Represent a decision that you are yet to make on a large sheet of art paper. Process by the usual means. Next create an image of what your world or life will be once the decision has been made and actioned. What will your world look like?

Remember this is not a depiction of your world with one clear answer or another, but your world generally. After the usual processing, leave the art works in view so you can continue to ponder the outcome.

# Finding peace

Another variation is for the client who has depicted a troubling situation over which he or she has little control, to then create a second artwork depicting what is needed to make peace with the situation.

Experiential task

Perhaps there is some element of your life at the moment, that although unpleasant, you cannot change. Use this situation and create a symbolic representation on a large art sheet.

Next, create an image that includes elements that provide some peace with the circumstance as it is.

As above, the solution may be nonsensical, but can still provide a sense of wellbeing or an image to recall when the situation seems overwhelming.

# Dialoguing with the art

A simple process that can be used with the art generated in a session is to establish a back and forth dialogue between the art and its creator.  The creator can ask questions of the art, where the art can respond as a voice, or as another art piece.  The art can also ask questions of the creator.

## CASE STUDY THREE

**Therapist:**  This image about finding a direction in your life is very detailed. Does this say something about you?  If I were to ask the art what it knows about you, how would it respond?

**Client:**  The art would say that I am a bit of a details person.  A bit of a perfectionist I guess.

**Therapist:**  Is the art making a compliment, a criticism or simply an observation here?

**Client:**  Probably a criticism actually.

**Therapist:**  Do you have something to say to the artwork about that?

**Client:**  Well, I'd tell it...

**Therapist:**  Why don't you tell it directly?

**Client:**  (Addressing the art) Ok. Well, it's fine for you to think that's bad but I've always been praised for getting things perfect. And I like praise.

**Therapist:**  And how does the art respond?

**Client:**  (As the art) Fine. You like praise and perfection but they aren't getting you a job. No one wants a professional perfectionist. You have to have some other skill.

**Client:**  (Addressing the art) Yes, but I don't know what. What will I do?  No job or career is right.  I guess I'm being a perfectionist in looking too aren't I?

**Client:**  (As the art) Well maybe you just have to do something. Don't worry if it's not the perfect job. Just do something.

**Client:**  (Addressing the art and the therapist) But that is just *so* not me.

**Therapist:**  Perhaps we can ask the art to show you what this might look like, being able to just do something but not lose the essential characteristics of your desire to get things perfect.

**Client:**  (Addressing the art) what do I need to do and how will I be able to do just something but not compromise my values?

(Client creates new image that is one step removed from her, but is a reflection of what the art believes is possible.)

There are many means and models for dialoguing with the art.  The essential component is in the externalisation and personification of the art piece.  If the art 'has an opinion' it can be utilised effectively.

Experiential task

Look over the many pieces of art you have already completed.  Ask yourself; does any particular piece have something to say to me?  Can I learn something by listening to this art piece?

It is useful when doing this activity alone, to take two different pieces of writing paper, and to jot down the comments and questions from yourself, and the art.  Make sure you name each page, as it is very likely you will get your own words mixed up with those of your art!

# Symbols of clarification

In examining the many facets of an issue and the client's experience of it, the use of a few selected symbols may be beneficial. The symbols that provide a basic set for exploration are heart, mind, body and soul. The client will initially create an image for each of these symbols, paying close attention to how the symbol speaks of their core beliefs about each. Once the four symbols are complete, (or more, if required), the client asks the symbol "What does my mind (or heart, body, soul), have to say about the problem?" and answers with another artwork. Each of these secondary art works must be approached individually for the clarity sought by employing such a technique. After each art creation, process each individually and then as a collective. Other symbols can be quite useful especially those archetypal symbols relevant to the client's issue and goal. For instance, a woman who feels constantly exhausted may find the 'mother' symbol relevant if she has children. A highly religious person may wish to have a relevant spiritual guide, for instance, a Christian may depict a cross for viewing the situation from God's perspective.

Another set of symbols that can be useful for clients who are familiar with Jung's elements of the psyche, are persona, ego, shadow, anima and animus, and the self. (Jung, 1999)

It is tempting to create a set of symbols and just 'whip out' the relevant few for a client when required. This is not advised. In order to consider and dwell with the perspective presented from one angle, the core beliefs and concepts regarding this element must first be defined. The creation of the symbol has as much healing or insight potential as the final task.

It may be useful to refer to a list such as the one below for other symbols that may be relevant to the client's work.

| | |
|---|---|
| Body | Wife/husband |
| Mind | Hero |
| Soul | Victim |
| Heart | Child |
| Spirit | Daughter/Son |
| Mother/Father | Wise old man |
| Crone | Family |
| Maiden | Best Friend |
| Master | Society |

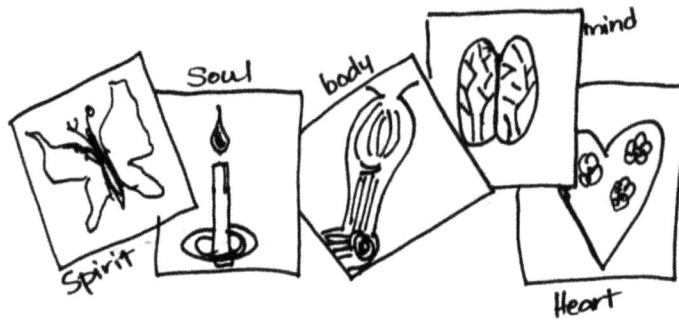

Going back to work after a baby arrives:

*Using symbols to enhance clarification of issue*

Experiential task

Create small symbols representing Jung's key five elements of the psyche, 'persona', 'ego', 'shadow', 'anima' and 'animus', and the 'self'. Use each of these symbols in turn to reflect upon where you are now in your life. How does 'shadow' work in your life today? How is 'anima and animus' expressed in your life?

Now choose an issue to explore using the four standard symbols for this exercise, heart, mind, body and soul. Again create the small symbols to begin, then create larger art works using the particular symbol chosen. For instance, "what does my heart have to say about my fear of flying?" and "What does my body say about my fear of flying?" and so on.
Remember to process each artwork that results.

**Further reading**

Rita Simon, *Symbolic Images in Art as Therapy*, 1997, Routledge

# Call and Response Process

Therapists creating art themselves within a client-centred Art Therapy model, is not common practice but does have a place, particularly in a 'Call and Response' art process. Whilst creating an image perhaps the client demonstrated a range of emotions and body language that the therapist can mirror. Just as paraphrasing is a valuable tool in verbal counselling, a reflective art piece that mirrors the client's pattern of behaviour during the art making, can be very useful. A new client may also have created an image and yet be somewhat tentative about disclosing information. In this case a reflective art piece can also be useful, provided you have taken sufficient notes to given authenticity to the mirroring. In order to avoid therapeutic violence however, it is important to approach this art making thoughtfully. It is important to check in with the client to ascertain that they are comfortable with watching you create a response. If the client approves, remember to still attend to your client even during your own art making.

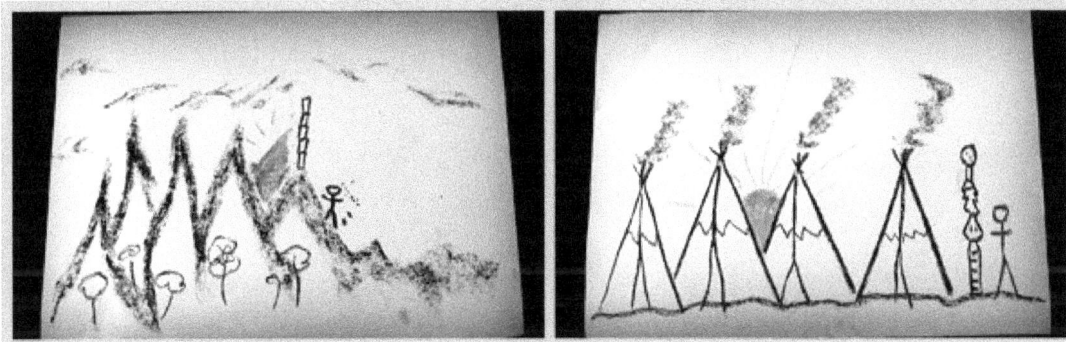

The client's 'call'                          The therapist's response

The primary task is to mirror the body language. Allow the emotion that you witnessed to show on your face also, but reduce its intensity a little. For instance, if the client cried, do not cry, but use a facial expression that indicates a deep sadness. Full-belly laughter can be mirrored using a big smile and a giggle. Remember with the art to be intuitively synchronous with what is expressed. Under no circumstances should you allow your beliefs regarding the issue, or image, and the possible resolutions for this to enter into your artwork. Simply respond with resonant shapes and colours, building an image and adding small elements for completion.

Upon completion, check in with the client to see if he or she is comfortable with what you have created.  If it has been confronting for the client, put it aside and explain that perhaps the feelings that caused the discomfort may be useful to explore at a later time. Most likely, the client will have watched you with an internal dialogue, testing, adjusting and making meaning for what he or she witnesses through your art making.  This is a similar response to paraphrasing. The client hears the statements, or sees the image, then checks for validity and adjusts the material to create greater accuracy or add further meaning.  This is a terrific approach when the client is reluctant to tell the therapist details about what the presenting issue is.

Experiential task

Take an earlier piece of your art.  Place it a great distance away and look at it in its original position and in rotation. Look for something you didn't intend. Notice the colours and shapes. Draw or paint an image that has resonance with the art itself, not the meanings attributed to it.

Now go back to the original intention in drawing the first image, place both art works side by side and see if you notice anything useful in the second image.

# Bi-lateral art process

Although vastly over-generalised, the notions of left and right brain function specialties is still valid, and forms the underlying justifications for bi-lateral Art Therapy. Neuroscientist, Gazzaniga, described the dominant functionality of the left hemisphere as cognitive problem solving, language, and speech. The right hemisphere was described as very poor at problem-solving, but good at visual/motor activities and holistic thinking (Gazzaniga, 1998) . Bi-lateral art processes aim to integrate the cognitive, visual and holistic specialities to create better awareness or acceptance of a specific issue.

The best issues for utilising this approach are where there is a difficult incompatibility with two clear possibilities/outcomes.

For example, "I want to be a good mother but feel it is just not possible to perform this role at a standard I would approve of myself for, whilst I am compelled to work fulltime. Do I work and feel like a bad Mum, or do I give up my work so I can feel I've done my best as a parent?"

Or

"My Christian beliefs strictly condemn certain behaviours yet this seems incongruent with living in this world"

Or

"My 16 year old daughter, who is living at home, sleeps with her boyfriend in our house and it feels wrong. I hate it, but I also feel that if I am strict and forbid it, she won't come home so often, she'll be forced to lie to me, and she'll still be sleeping with him anyway."

The following details the steps in one approach to bi-lateral work.

Have the client decide which hand owns which outcome.

Place two pages side by side in front of the client. He/she will use the same pages repeatedly, so use a good quality, heavy paper. Tape these pages to the table surface to prevent slippage while working.

Work only on one page at a time, keeping it in the original position.

Use paint and no brushes, only fingers. This may initially feel uncomfortable, but once the client begins, this will almost certainly be fun and relaxing. It is important to have a clear sensory experience to really facilitate left/right brain activation in balance.

Throughout the activity ask the client to allow thoughts to surface regarding the issue.

Ask the client to choose which outcome to begin to work with first. Use the hand assigned to this decision to create a flowing (not detailed) picture that is colour and shape, probably without form or with simple symbols. Keep working it with this one hand, over and over until the client loses the awareness of the paper and process and just feels it in his/her body.

Swap to the other page. Use the other hand, to work with the other outcome as per the previous hand, leaving the page at the side of the body that corresponds to the hand currently being used.

Swap to the other page again but this time use the right hand to paint the right hand outcome on the left hand page. Leave the paper in its original position. Keep working it with this one hand, over and over until the client loses the awareness of the paper and process and just feels it in his/her body.

Swap pages again, using the left hand to paint the left hand outcome on the right hand page. Leave the paper in its original position. Keep working it with this one hand, over and over until the client loses the awareness of the paper and process and just feels it in his/her body.

Now using both hands at once and crossed over, ask the client to allow his or her hands to find symmetry in the images, one that both hands can work with in a synchronised movement. Leave the papers in the original position. Keep working with both hands at once in a synchronised pattern, allowing the awareness of the paint and paper to drop away and to feel a coming together of all the knowledge and understanding you have of the possibilities. Perhaps a dominant shape, colour or symbol appears. Does this have some information for you about how you might view the issue identified? What might it mean?

Remember the client is activating imagination and curiosity, gathering together the left and right brain functions at once - the holistic, intuitive, visual and cognitive. This optimises opportunity for new insight, so do not dismiss the weird and wonderful ideas that might present.

Remind the client to relax and breathe deeply, and to enjoy the freedom in this activity. Also remind him or her that this activity is certainly not about the product.

Perhaps no concrete or useful information or resolution will present to the client immediately, but over the following week or so, a new approach might become evident as the client's unconscious works overtime at trying to integrate the information and make some peace with the outcome.

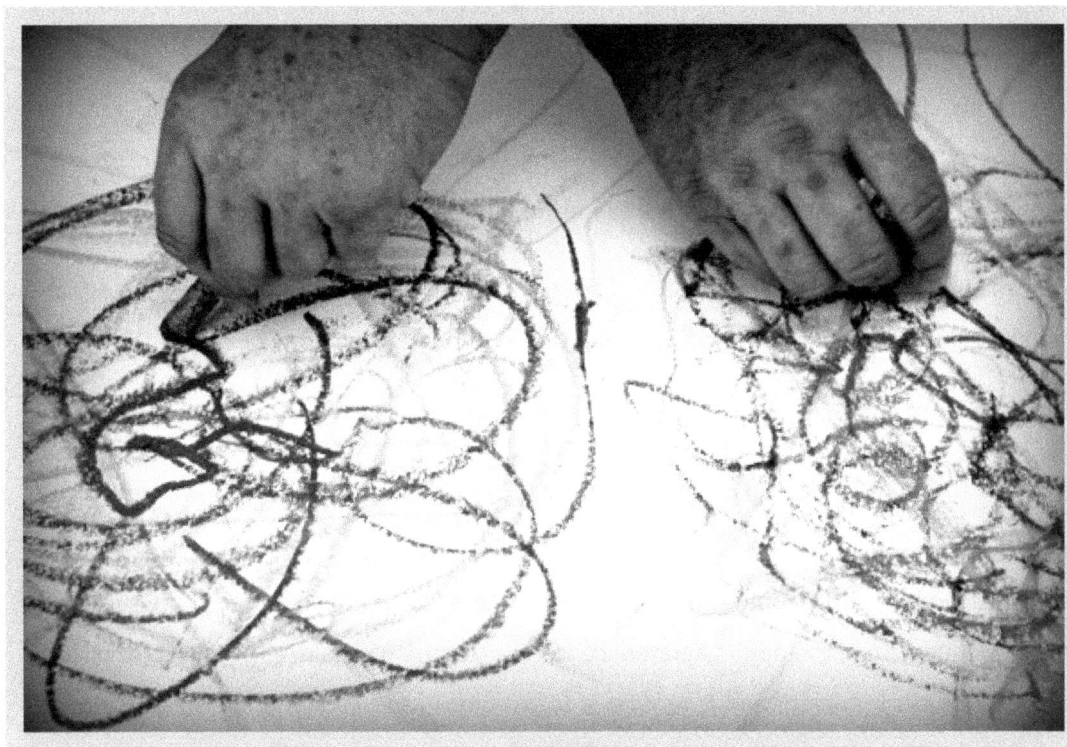

Experiential task

Choose a current issue to work with. The best issues for utilising this approach are where there is a difficult incompatibility with two clear possibilities or outcomes. Follow the bilateral protocol above and simply trust the process.

Be alert to dreams or flashes of insight that occur over the next few weeks.

**Further Reading**

Doris Banowsky Arrington, *Art, Angst, and Trauma: Right Brain Interventions With Developmental Issues*, 2007, Charles C Thomas Publishers ltd.

# Totems

Totems are animals, plants or natural objects that serve as an emblem of a family, clan, or belief system. These can also act as reminders of ancestry. The object totem is often a carved, sculpted or painted representation of such emblems. These objects can also act as pages in a storybook, often containing rich information.  Different cultures around the world have used totems for centuries to signify different clan and tribes, to declare specific roles for individuals, and to celebrate special events.  Native American Indians have constructed totem poles to document and celebrate marriage, significant historical events and the death of great leaders.

There are many times within therapy that a client will reflect upon family, belonging, ancestral traits and belief systems.  At these times, constructing a personal totem may be of great value in healing.

# Carving

Carving wood can be a difficult and time-consuming process, but there are other, more suitable options for limited time therapy.  Aerated concrete, (commonly sold as 'Hebel blocks' in Australia) is very easily carved, and a 30 x 20 x 20 cm block can be carved in a basic style in roughly 2 hours with basic woodworking tools.  Carving is a wonderful activity for any client who is very quick and certain about things in his or her life.  It may be that this ability to quickly find solutions is hindering his or her ability to think deeper about a situation and find other possibilities. Because carving takes considerable time, the client is slowed down, and dwells with the issue for a longer period than he or she would do if asked to talk about the situation.  This can provide a wonderful window for all of the known answers to have been ruminated over, and for new possibilities to begin to emerge.  Many men also find carving useful as it is less feminised than other art forms. It also uses traditionally masculine tools with which they may be familiar and carving requires some physical energy that can be affirming for men in therapy.

Remember, this style of art process is removing and chipping away at the object and thus it is important to consider this quality when offering this medium. Does it resonate with the client's experience, or does it challenge them?  If the client is seeking to let go of old, destructive habits this may be very useful. If however a client is seeking to develop trust and allow people more entry to his or her world then a process of building something would be recommended, rather than an act of 'taking away'.

Experiential task

Gather together a few simple carving tools, some sandpaper and a small piece of aerated concrete. Be sure to use a dust mask and complete this activity in a well-ventilated area. Carve an object symbolic of your family. It may be heraldic in nature, something like a coat of arms, or it may be more like a mini America Indian totem pole, or an amulet, an object designed to protect your family from troubles.

What thoughts and emotions surfaced during this activity?

# Construction

Where a building quality is preferable over 'taking away', a totem object that can be constructed by adding material may serve the goal more effectively. To do this, use an armature on which to build a sculpture or totem.  This can be easily created by placing sticks in a small container - a milk carton, or yoghurt container - into which is poured wet casting plaster, or even sand. Support the sticks in a balanced and upright position until the plaster has set. The container can then be cut away, or left in place.  This armature is wonderful for using with small objects, natural, or found, and with an assortment of simple store bought materials.

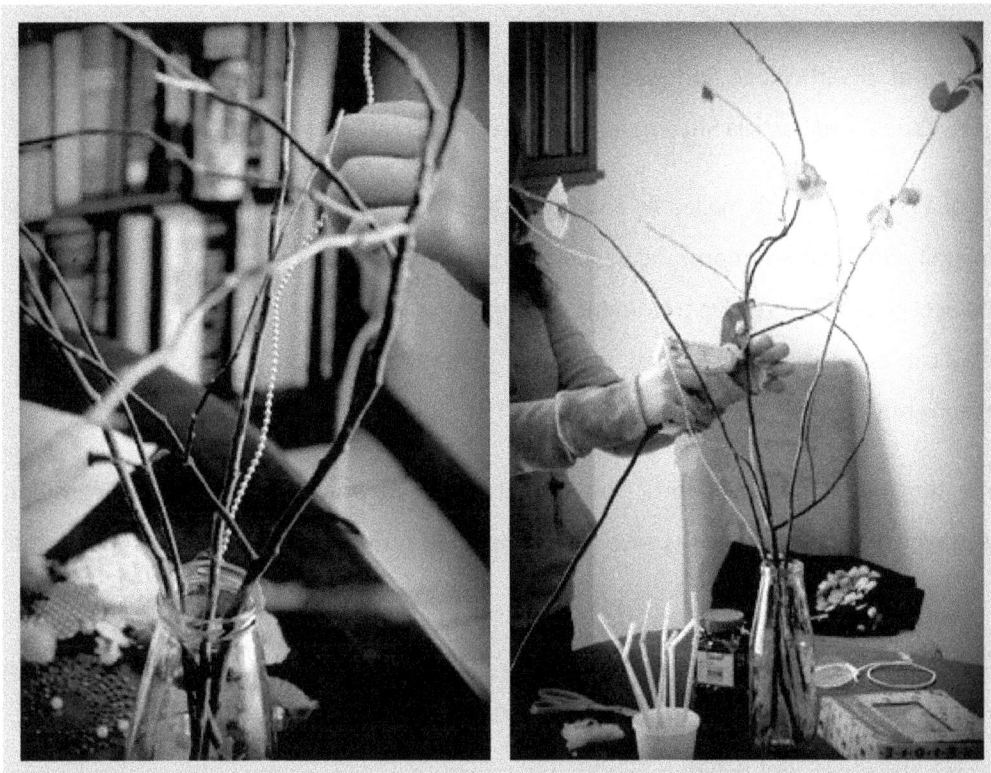

A hot glue gun is required to quickly and easily attach the objects to the frame. This frame has many opportunities to express experience in three dimensions. Perhaps the client adds objects in the upper levels of the armature representing details of paramount importance or as a projection into the future. Lower areas on the armature may represent bedrock/foundational issues or perhaps minor insignificant elements. Foreground and background can be used purposefully, and with rotation the opportunity to see through the creation from many angles, reflecting on how one perspective may block or enhance another.

Experiential task

Find a large jar, pot or vase. Fill the bottom with sand and push into it some sticks. If you do not have this equipment readily available, use a plastic cup, some salt and a few straws. A hot glue gun is essential for this activity as it allows the glue to dry very quickly. Gather together a bowl full of objects, found and bought, along with some string or wool.

Use this armature to create a 'totem' representing your friendships.
When you have finished remember to process this artwork as you would a drawn picture.
Rotate the object, move it far away, ask yourself, "What do I see?"
Note how the creation of this object has helped you think about friendships in your life.

# Clay

Clay is another three-dimensional art medium that lends itself to the therapeutic context very well. It is not at all difficult to find resources for working therapeutically with clay. Books by David Henley (2002) and Patricia Sherwood (2004) are terrific references for this work.

Clay has a quality that is both malleable and grounding. The earthy smell and colour can draw out and magnify the basic emotions. Adolescents in particular seem to respond to the medium's capacity to accept quite aggressive treatment, through banging, squashing, bending or breaking it. The clay can be readily transformed, mirroring perhaps an internal transformation that is desired or currently being experienced.

When reflecting upon the qualities of this medium, it is extremely important to consider situations in which the medium may prove too challenging for the client at a particular point in therapy.

This medium is best not used until the client has disclosed something of his or her story. The medium can very quickly draw experiences of sexual abuse to the surface, possibly overwhelming the client and creating psychic resistance. Other experiences may also have a strong resonance with clay, especially for those involved in warfare. This does not mean that clay cannot be used with these clients, but that this will be done at an appropriate point and with great care. Clay is such a powerful medium yet must be very carefully considered before using in therapy with any client.

"ah person", Ky Alecto, 2008

Experiential task

Consider your transitions from adolescent to adult. Spend at least 10 minutes just moulding the clay and becoming comfortable with it. When you are ready, allow the clay to form into an object symbolic of your adolescent years. When this stage is complete, wash your hands, move around and then come back to the symbol. Process as usual. Next, close your eyes for a few moments and recall the transition you made into adulthood.

What shifted within you? Allow your hands to take the adolescent object and transform it into your adult self. Try not to over-think this creation and just allow something to appear. How did the action of moulding the clay, resonate with your sense of transformation from one stage to the next?

**Further Reading**

Patricia Sherwood, *The Healing Art of Clay Therapy*, 2004, Acer Press

# Mask Work

The word 'mask' is used in many contexts. It may be used to denote an actual object that conceals one face in order to display another, or it may be used in reference to "masking off", that is concealing one area in order to protect it. The word is used extensively in therapy in reference to any part of the persona or psyche, which is concealed, by the use of some psychological device. These concealed parts of ourselves may also be masked, and may be psychologically healthy to expose, or unhealthy. It is in the ability to comfortably and appropriately manipulate one's many masks that psychological health is obtained. The drama therapist Robert Landy hints at this when he proposes that perhaps there is no 'self'; that perhaps we are all merely a sum of roles which we either play well or not so well (Landy, 1996).

Mask, in terms of the psychological device, is necessary to some degree, in successful social interaction. If we were to be always expressing our authenticity, we may be offensive, patronising or just downright insensitive to others. In a very simplified example, if I am socialising with a friend whose baby has recently died, my joy at the impending birth of another grandchild may need to be masked somewhat to allow my friend the safety in our relationship of not being too confronted by the reality of joy existing when her own world is so bleak. In the event that I am suffering, I will also mask some of my sadness when attending a joyous celebration. Our social competence depends upon this ability to moderate and conceal, to escalate and reveal, when the timing and environment is right. Think for a moment about some of the people you know who "let it all hang out", or those people whose beliefs and values are constantly on display. Our need in society to mask is clear when I hear adolescents using the phrase, "suck it up", often accompanied by "princess", as if whoever is being addressed is acting as if he or she is somehow more entitled to outrage or despair than the average person. The "sucking it up" process is one of masking. A lack of competence in mask manipulation in this simple sense can be seen often in people who have an Autism Spectrum Disorder. This is often a result of impaired theory of mind (the ability to view things from another's perspective,) but can also arise from the individual's unwillingness to be anything other than fully authentic in the moment.

Of course, mask wearing can be an unhealthy psychological habit. Unhealthy mask wearing commonly falls into two categories. The first is when the wearer uses the mask to conceal his or her own authenticity, not to protect others, but to protect oneself in ways that limit self-worth, self-acceptance and fulfilment. The second unhealthy mask is the mask worn when the wearer is unaware of the mask's existence.  This is subconscious material playing out, perhaps in a model of Jung's shadow material, or Freud's death instinct.

The aim in all mask work is the regulation and integration of disowned parts of one's personality.

Mask work in therapy can be a confronting and powerful medium.  It is not advised unless the therapeutic relationship is strong, and the client stable with easy access to immediate supports (friends, family, mental health service), if required.


## CASE STUDY FOUR

**Therapist:**    Jeanette, every now and again, I hear a little voice, just pop up in your dialogue. It sounds like a different or perhaps a younger version of you.  Two phrases I've heard and noted here are "But I want to" and "it's really not that simple".  I wonder if there is a different version of you that has a different viewpoint?

**Jeanette:**    Yeah, like I hear everything I say, and I do believe it, but there are these bits that are just bursting to get out of me. I hear them and they are stupid though.

**Therapist:**    So no matter how hard you try to suppress that voice, it just keeps popping into the conversation?

**Jeanette:**    Yes.  I know it's wrong to listen to it.  I don't know why I'm so determined to screw it up.

**Therapist:**    I wonder if this voice just needs to be heard for a few moments? Remember you can listen to something without actioning its advice.  Would you feel comfortable just letting this voice speak, without having to pay heed to what it says?

**Jeanette:**    Yeah. I think so.

**Therapist:**    I am also interested in what the character looks like that has this voice.  Perhaps some of this character's features might help us understand why he or she is so determined to drop these statements into your dialogue.  I have this plain mask frame here and I am wondering if you could just imagine for a moment, if this voice had a face, what it might look like.  Can you create this face here?

(Therapist provides client with array of construction and art materials).

**Jeanette:**    There is a different feeling when those thoughts come out of my mouth.

**Therapist:**    Let's take a few minutes to get in touch with those feelings shall we?

**Jeanette:**    Sure.

| Therapist: | Sit back in your chair, in a comfortable position and focus for a moment on your breathing. Allow your eyes to close gently. Just feel the breath gently pulled in, feel your tummy just slightly rise and then allow the breath to steadily, evenly slip out and feel your tummy fall. Just focus on this rhythm for a moment or two. Put aside for a moment, this wise Jeanette, and just give the other voice some time and air space. Know that just because this voice makes a comment that doesn't fit your goal, it's ok; you don't need to do what this voice suggests, just listen. Where does this voice begin in your body? Find that place and just allow all your attention to rest on that place. Listen now to the voice as it says, "it's not really that simple". What are the feelings that push these words out of you? No need to tell me, just pay attention to you. What face does this person have? What are the feelings present on this face? How do these feelings create the expression? When you are ready, open your eyes and put those colours shapes and images that come to you into this mask. Put those feelings into the facial expression. |
|---|---|
| Jeanette: | (works away silently for approx 15 mins) There – there she is! |
| Therapist: | So let's look at her. |
| Jeanette: | She seems like a spoilt child, but she's afraid too. |
| Therapist: | Do you think you could wear her for a few moments at a time to really understand her? You can use the mirror to see her better. |
| Jeanette: | (Under the mask) This is weird. I feel a bit stupid. |
| Therapist: | Lucky it's just you and me hey? I promise not to tell anyone! What do you see when you look at her? |
| Jeanette: | It's weird. She looks, mmm what's the word? Petulant. But I think I can see in her eyes that she is scared. Stupid hey, because it's my own eyes I can see through the holes! |
| Therapist: | Jeanette, take the mask off for a moment and look at yourself. What do YOU want to ask the mask? |
| Jeanette: | Well I'd like to know why it wants me to fail and give up. |
| Therapist: | Hold that mask up alongside you, and looking into the reflection in the mirror, make eye contact with the mask as you ask it. Start with " Why do you...?" |
| Jeanette: | (Addressing the mask) Why do you want me to screw it up? |
| Therapist: | Slip the mask up in front of your face and she how it answers. |
| Jeanette: | (As Mask) This is dumb. I feel like crying. I'm sorry. (Pulls the mask away) |
| Therapist: | (After a pause whilst the client composes herself) Gosh, this mask seems to have some powerful hold of your emotions. |
| Jeanette: | Yes, and it is silly because it's just paper and paint and this stuff stuck on it. |

| | |
|---|---|
| **Therapist:** | So it's silly, but emotive anyway? Perhaps it is like a key to some usually unexpressed feelings? |
| **Jeanette:** | Yes. And I want to get to the bottom of it. Do you think doing this will help? |
| **Therapist:** | Doing this might help but it's your call. Do you want to continue with this? |
| **Jeanette:** | Yes, yeah. Give me a minute. (Jeanette pulls tissues close, pulls her chair forward and straightens her back, indicating a determination to proceed) I'm ready. |
| **Therapist:** | Let's try this again. You want to know from the mask why it wants you to 'screw up'. Try asking the mask again, then slip the mask on and respond. |
| **Jeanette:** | (Addressing the mask) Why do you want me to screw it up? |
| **Jeanette:** | (As mask) I don't want a relationship with anybody. |
| **Jeanette:** | (Removing the mask and addressing the therapist) But that's not true really, I DO, I DO, there is just something in the corner making me get these stupid feelings. It's like there is a monster in my head. |
| **Therapist:** | And this is ok for now. Remember we are going to give this voice some time. I believe you when you tell me that you want this relationship. I am listening to what the other voice has to say, but we can debate what's truth and what's not after. How does that sound? |
| **Jeanette:** | Ok then. |
| **Therapist:** | Try to imagine this other voice as separate from the 'real you'. Hopefully this will help you feel less like you need to defend yourself against the mask. |
| **Jeanette:** | (Addressing the mask) Ok, so YOU don't want a relationship with somebody. Why not? |
| **Jeanette:** | (As mask) It's just giving in to all the romance novels you've read, thinking that a relationship will be a happy ever after thing. |
| **Jeanette:** | (Pauses – addressing the mask) So is there something wrong with that? Why can't I believe that I'll live happily ever after? Maybe I will. |
| **Jeanette:** | (As the mask) You know that is ridiculous. You'll never be able to make this work. |
| **Jeanette:** | (Addressing the mask) But this is why I am here. I will do everything I can to make this relationship work. We'll get professional help, I'll do all the right things and it WILL work. |
| **Jeanette:** | (As the mask) You are kidding yourself. Relationships don't work. Look at everyone around you. |
| | NOTE    (Here is where integration begins) |

| | |
|---|---|
| **Jeanette:** | (Addressing the mask and the therapist- begins to cry) It's true. I am SO scared. My brain thinks it can work with the right help but here (pointing to her heart) I am scared it won't. And it will hurt so much if it doesn't work. It will. I've seen it before. |
| **Therapist:** | (with gentle encouragement) Keep trying here, keep up the communication, maybe you can help one another. |
| **Jeanette:** | (Addressing the mask) But I want this to work so badly. I'll do anything. |
| **Jeanette:** | (As the mask)    That's not true.  When Ryan asked you to go to his work Christmas thing, I said "no". |
| **Therapist:** | Remember to keep the mask and your own statements separate, try "You said 'no'." |
| **Jeanette:** | (As the mask) You said 'no' to Ryan when he asked you to go.  You won't do everything. Sometimes you hold a bit back. You had no good reason to say 'no'. But you did. |
| **Jeanette:** | (Addressing the mask) I just didn't want to go. |
| **Jeanette:** | (As the mask) And you shouldn't have gone.  It was the right decision. |
| **Jeanette:** | No hang on. I SHOULD have gone. It's just that YOU didn't want to go. |
| **Jeanette:** | (As the mask) That's right. I don't want to. So there. |
| **Jeanette:** | (Addressing the mask and the therapist) That just makes me really sad.  This is really dumb; I should be working together on this. - Phew that doesn't make sense.  If sometimes I listen to you, and other times to me, then we'll really mess it up.  Why can't you just believe? Believe that we CAN make this work? |
| **Jeanette:** | (As the mask) It's not that simple. You know that relationships don't work out. How often have you seen this? |
| **Jeanette:** | (Addressing the mask) Alright, alright, maybe it won't work out. |
| | (Jeanette pauses and begins to cry again) |
| **Jeanette:** | (Addressing the therapist) I think I'd just die if I screw this one up. I couldn't live with myself. |
| **Therapist:** | So is the mask just trying to save you from self destruction? |
| **Jeanette:** | I think so, yes.  That bit of me just can't take the risk that it won't work out. |
| **Therapist:** | Does that mean that the other part of you can take the risk? |
| **Jeanette:** | No actually, I don't believe anywhere that I can risk being broken hearted again. I guess I'm just refusing to go there. Refusing to think about it.  Well, mostly, except for that mask bit of me. |

| | |
|---|---|
| **Therapist:** | OK. So do you think the more you push away those thoughts, the more determined they are to surface, because you aren't listening to them? Do they even get sneaky and pop out in different ways like not attending Ryan's Christmas function? Does this sound right? |
| **Jeanette:** | Yes, but to listen to those feelings means I don't even try. I DO want this relationship. I just want it for forever. |
| **Therapist:** | The mask seems to be saying though that you won't survive a broken heart and that there is just too great a risk that the relationship won't last. What do you think? |
| **Jeanette:** | It's a risk I'm prepared to take. |
| **Therapist:** | So you are willing to risk being hurt in order to have a relationship with Ryan? |
| **Jeanette:** | Yes. But it is so scary to think about. |
| **Therapist:** | Ok, it's really scary. Can you acknowledge the mask's fear and concerns for you in some more dialogue? |
| **Jeanette:** | (Addressing the mask) I know you are afraid, and I can understand that. After what happened with Jonathon, I am shit scared too. Mum and Dad nearly killed each other, Nan and Pop were horrendous, and Gran's husband died on her. Christy and Sandra and Evan have all had screwed up relationships that didn't last. I guess it is easy to wonder if it's something in your genes. But we'll never know if we might be the ones to beat the odds eh? Maybe we are the ones meant to break this curse. If I don't try I'll never know and maybe I'll miss out on something truly beautiful. |
| **Jeanette:** | (As the mask) It's just not that simple though. It'll be great if it works, but what if it doesn't. How will we survive? How will I ever be able to face getting up again? |
| **Jeanette:** | (Addressing the mask) Well... I don't know and I don't want to think about it. (Long pause) I guess, if it happens, well, I will always have Christy to go to. I guess I can get help then. I'll be devastated but I suppose I'd survive it. It's not like I haven't seen people broken hearted but eventually get their life together again. I suppose I'll just have to hope that I'll be ok. Because if I don't hope I'll be ok in a breakup, I'll never try. |
| **Jeanette:** | (As the mask) Well, be warned, it'll hurt if it doesn't work. You need to have a plan of how you'll cope. You'll need to keep believing you'll manage. |
| **Jeanette:** | (Addressing the mask) I can do that. I won't be planning to breakup, but I'll be planning to be strong no matter what. I'll accept the risk. |
| **Therapist:** | Is there something you want to tell the mask before we finish with it today? |

**Jeanette:** (Addressing the mask) Ok. I hear you. I'm prepared to be hurt if necessary, but I'm not going to let this fear ruin my chance to experience something that could be really amazing, and could last a lifetime. Ok?

**Therapist:** So wow. What a conversation... (Continues and supports the client back to the temporal world and reviews the material that presented)

**Therapist:** When you are ready I'd like you to think about what you want to do with this mask. Do you want to keep it, destroy it, photograph or frame it? Think about how it will serve you best.

Experiential task

Consider an internal voice you have that seldom gets heard in your day-to-day living, or is perhaps repeatedly put down in your internal dialoguing. Commit to giving this voice a face, to create the face or mask that is usually hidden. Although some 'voices' might be a little frightening, often once they have been fully heard, they will fade away.

Once you have created the 'seldom heard' mask, use a mirror to create a dialogue between you without this mask, and you with this mask.
How did this activity support integration of this seldom heard voice?

**Further Reading**

Les Barbanell, *Removing the Mask of Kindness: Diagnosis and Treatment of the Caretaker Personality Disorder*, 2006, Jason Aronson

Sue Jennings and Ase Minde  *Art Therapy and Dramatherapy: Masks of the Soul*, 1994 Jessica Kingsley

# Empty chair work

A Gestalt therapist, will often use a technique utilizing an 'empty chair'. The Empty Chair technique was developed and popularized by Frederick (Fritz) Pearls (Nichol & Schwartz, 2008).

Empty chair exercises work well within an Art Therapy model, especially when using an artefact or image created in therapy in the empty chair.

The technique is frequently used if a client expresses a conflict with another person. The client is directed to talk to the other person who is imagined to be sitting in the empty chair. This helps the client to experience and understand his or her feelings and those of the other person more fully. The therapist may say, "Imagine your sister in this chair. See her sitting there, and, now talk to her about how you felt when she tried to kill herself."

This technique can just as easily be used for art products (a portrait of someone, a representation of a situation), or personified objects (a parchment speaking for academic achievements or a walking stick representing a health challenge), for parts of your personality (critical parent, the shy child, workaholic), any of your emotions, symptoms (pain, disease or headache), or any aspect of a dream. Success depends upon a detailed and emotional interaction in the form of a conversation.

The client shifts back and forth from the client's chair, to the empty chair, responding from the perspective of the person (or other aspect) using first person dialogue. This is similar to the mask work, however this technique is more suitable for dialoguing with persons other than self. This technique can be very useful in resolving past issues, especially where the other party is deceased or is no longer in the client's life.

Again, this is not a technique to be used with people who are emotionally flooded, as it would be too overwhelming and likely to result in distress or psychic resistance. This is a technique extremely useful for clients who are less able to imagine a situation from another's perspective, or have become stuck in a single view of the situation.

# CASE STUDY FIVE

**Therapist:**   John, you have done an enormous amount of work around the choices you made when confronted by so many people in immediate need. You made choices that you believe reflected the best ethical decision you could make. This resulted in two people dying, and four living. You worked strenuously to do all you could in the 30 minutes before the ambulance arrived. With no one else in sight and on an incredibly hot day you had to make quick decisions, even after the shock you experienced yourself.   After the work we have done, we still hear that distressed other voice coming through, that voice that advocates for that man and his little daughter. When we empathise with someone we put ourselves in the other person's life and experience, and test how it feels for us. I know this has been extremely painful for you to do. I am wondering though, if rather than just feeling the pain, if you might imagine the thinking too. What would that man have done himself, given the circumstances? I am wondering if you could put him here, in this chair, and for a few minutes just talk to him. Have a conversation back and forth about what happened. If at any point this gets too difficult, we can stop. How does this sound?

**John:**   Sure, I can do that.

**Therapist:**   So in this chair, we have Christopher. The man you believed him to be, still able to reflect on what occurred. What do you want to say to him?

**John:**   (As himself) Um, Christopher. I'm sorry man that I couldn't do anything for you. I mean, I didn't think you were even alive when I first saw you. I'm so sorry. And about your little girl. Oh My God, she looked so perfect, so beautiful from the shoulders up. I couldn't imagine for a minute that she would live. And the others just kept yelling. Oh God, I'm sorry.

**Therapist:**   John, when you are ready, just slip over into Christopher's seat. When you feel ready you can reply to John.

**John:**   (As Christopher) I want to be angry with you but I can't. I'm mostly angry at you for my wife's sake, and our boys. I think they deserved something better than those jackasses taking us away from the family. I'm pissed you saved the jackasses lives, but couldn't save my daughter.

**John:**   (As himself) It all happened so quickly, I couldn't think. You know I didn't really even know what happened. I just drove over the hill and there were three cars just mashed together, and the wheels still spinning, like I just didn't think. I just jammed on the skids jumped out and thought 'how can I help?' I looked at the little girl first. She seemed so innocent in all this, and I just couldn't go to her. She wasn't awake and I truly thought she'd be dead, or really very, very soon, and just a bit of me went "I can't do anything for her". And really, I don't know what I could have done. I'm sorry man, I'm sorry.

| | |
|---|---|
| **John:** | Slowly walks to the other chair – as Christopher) You know man, I understand. I guess it was a hell of a shock. I guess it's not like you're trained in this sort of thing. You've just done a senior first aid course. I don't think you could have saved either of us anyway. I just wished you'd held her hand or something, been with her when she died. |
| **John:** | I have to believe that I did the right thing. I just acted on instinct, and when that guy was hysterical, thinking his car would go up in smoke, I knew he had a chance, I knew I had to do something then. I rang ooo screaming into my phone on my shoulder as I found something to break the window. Once he was out and the other guy helped me tie his leg so it wasn't bleeding so much, well, then I had a few minutes. I ran to my car and drove it to the crest of the hill to stop other cars crashing into us, not that there had been even one on that road. I went back to the groaning guy. You know he was conscious and it felt like that was where I needed to go. But the second he started bleating on about the other idiots smashing up his car; I knew I didn't want to help him. Selfish bastard never asked about how anyone else was, his mates, or you guys. Then I went to you, you didn't look so bad, just a funny shape, I'm sorry man. Then I ran to your girl. Her eyes flickered and I thought, oh my God, she's alive. I tried to pack my shirt into the spots that were bleeding, but man, I didn't know what to do for her. I just didn't know. I ran back to the others who could move and asked them if they knew anything, if they could help. I rang ooo again and asked them. I paced and looked for the ambulance but nothing, nothing helped. I ran back to my car to see if I had any spare clothes to use, and when I got back she was gone. She wasn't breathing man. (Sob) Your little girl had gone. I sat down on the ground next to her. I just wondered if you were her Dad and if she'd gone to be with you. Yeah man, I don't pray usually, but I did then, I said, 'oh god let her dad be helping her wherever she is now'. |
| **Therapist:** | (After a pause) Continue when you are ready and from which ever chair you need John. |
| **John:** | (As Christopher) Um, Thanks for telling me about it. I don't know how you could have done any better. I would've done the same. You're ok man. You're ok. |
| **John:** | (To therapist) I just wish I could give him a man hug you know? Shake his hand and stuff. I want to wish him well, which sounds ridiculous but there you go, it feels right. |
| **Therapist:** | John, you have said that you believe he and his daughter are in a better place. You do believe in life after death. If Christopher was able to see you actions now, would you like me to stand in for Christopher, so you can give him a man hug? (John is nodding). Tell me, what would you like me to say or do. |
| **John:** | I do think now that he's probably forgiven me. Could you tell me that it is ok? That I'm ok in what I did? |

(Therapist puts aside notes and moves to the 'empty' chair. John stands, therapist as Christopher stands. John extends his hand and leans in for a man hug. The therapist (as Christopher) takes John's hand and gives it a firm and generous shake and leans in for the man hug.)

**John:** (Addressing the therapist as Christopher) I am so sorry man

**Therapist:** (As Christopher) It's ok man, I forgive you. I know you did everything you could. Thanks for all you tried to do. You're all right you know mate; you're fine by me.

**John:** (Addressing the therapist as Christopher) Best of luck for you and your kid mate. I wish you the best whatever that is.

**Therapist:** (As Christopher) You too man. You have the best life, you're a great bloke.

(John and Therapist drop hands).

**John:** (Addressing therapist) Wow. I don't really know how but that just felt so good, like it's lifted so much from my shoulders.

Experiential task

Consider a person with whom you have some unresolved business. Be sure to close the curtains so the neighbours don't think poorly of you, and conduct an out loud dialogue between yourself and this imagined person in the empty chair.
How has this act altered your thoughts and feelings about this unfinished business?

**Further Reading**

Janie Rhyne, *The gestalt art experience: Creative process & expressive therapy*, 1984 Magnolia Street Publishers

# Three Step Art Process

There are many techniques that can be used alongside the more traditional approaches in therapy such as Cognitive Behavioural Therapy, Acceptance and Commitment Therapy, Mindfulness or even the less well known, such as Morita Therapy.

A three-step art process can be an effective tool in a Cognitive Behavioural Therapy approach, in any situation where the client believes he or she has little or no power to change the circumstance.

**STEP ONE**

The client creates a simple image about the circumstance, including him or herself somewhere in the image. This is to be completed in one colour only.

**STEP TWO**

The client creates a copy of the first image, same colours, shapes and lines with nothing changed and is then asked to add just one colour and one (or perhaps two) images representing actions or thoughts that can give him or her just a little more peace with the situation. Just as the client believes the circumstance cannot be change, so the first image cannot be adjusted, only added to. Nothing can be taken away.

**STEP THREE**

The client creates an exact copy again - this time, of Image TWO. Once complete the therapist asks the client to add as many colours, shapes and images as he or she can think of, that are representations of actions or thoughts that would make the situation as bearable as possible to give the client as much peace as feasible with the situation. Once again, as the circumstance is unchangeable, the original image cannot be taken away from, only added to.

The client can experience significant insight about how his or her thinking or actions can lead to less anxiety about the situation. The images cause the client to dwell with the situation, and can give the client something more tangible with which to imagine change. For instance, building a wall with other more positive beliefs in the image can assist the client in a critical situation as he or she recalls the physically constructed wall, in order to create the psychic defence.

Experiential task

Complete the 3-step process outlined above for a situation in which you have little or no control.  Avoid huge themes such as 'world peace'.
How did this act of creation assist in developing a new way of perceiving the situation?

**Further Reading**

Suzanne Degges-White and Nancy L. Davis, *Integrating the Expressive Arts into Counseling Practice: Theory-Based Interventions*, 2010 Springer Publishing

# Inner Child Work

Over the past 40 years many activities under the title of "Inner Child Work" have been developed. All aim to reintegrate the child into the adult psyche. Inner child work can allow for healing of childhood suffering and despair and can greatly assist in improving self worth and acceptance. Most recent forms of inner child work draw on the left and right brain theories, postulating that the use of both dominant and non-dominant handwork provides greater access to childhood memories and to facilitating integration. Inner child work also has a significant foot in the realm of transactional analysis, where the process uses ego-states to create distinction between adult, child and parent self, and to examine the exchanges in internal dialogue.

Although inner child work was first noted for mainstream therapy in the 1970s, the first use of the term in this context may have been in the marriage guidance book by W. Hugh Missildine M.D. in 1963, titled "Your Inner Child of the Past" (Missildine, 1991).

Recently, inner child work in an Art Therapy model has been popularised by authors such as Lucia Capacchione and Cathryn Taylor.

This exercise requires the therapist to have identified an age at which the client possesses unconditional positive regard for him or herself. Unconditional Positive Regard is a term first popularised by Carl Rogers, which refers the complete acceptance, support and value of a person regardless of what this person says or does. (Rogers, 1961) For some clients this may be an easy task, as he or she may believe that regardless of the mischief and mistakes that he or she was responsible for at aged 5, that this child was still wonderful and deserving of all life's possibilities, regardless of any minor flaws. Another client may however hold themselves responsible for many events, even in their earliest childhood. Children who have been sexually abused often place some or all of the blame upon themselves. Another client will consider that they were perhaps the baby that destroyed their parent's relationship. Even at birth it may be difficult to consider this baby with unconditional positive regard. Anytime from in utero (preferably in the later weeks to enable the creation of an image to which the client can relate) and up to five or six years of age is a good place to begin this work.

Prepare a large A2 or A3 art paper on an easel at eye level, or taped to a wall. If it is difficult for the client to create the artwork in this position, it can be completed on a tabletop and transferred to the wall or easel for the second step. Provide crayons, oil pastels or soft chalky pastels for this exercise to resonate with the childlike qualities that are desirous in the process. Do not use charcoal, pencils or markers as these have other qualities that may block the flow. Paint is not advised as it is slow to dry, can run, requires spill-able water, and can generally draw clients away from the child-like freedom required.

Explain to the client that you would like him or her to work with the non-dominant hand in this artwork. Explain that this will facilitate connection to the child within, that it will give the art work more childlike qualities and will to some degree discourage the pursuit of an excellent life-like portrait.

A guided visualisation in which the client is supported to journey back through time and to see him or herself as a child, to see the surroundings and the people is extremely helpful as a precursor to the art making.

Have the client create an image of him or herself as a child at the appointed age. Use a paper quality where detail can be added to the portrait. Encourage the image to be primarily the child, not backgrounds or other objects or people. Small but very significant objects (e.g. "the blue teddy that never left my side"), can be included if it enhances the client's intimacy with the artwork. The child's image needs a clear face for this exercise.

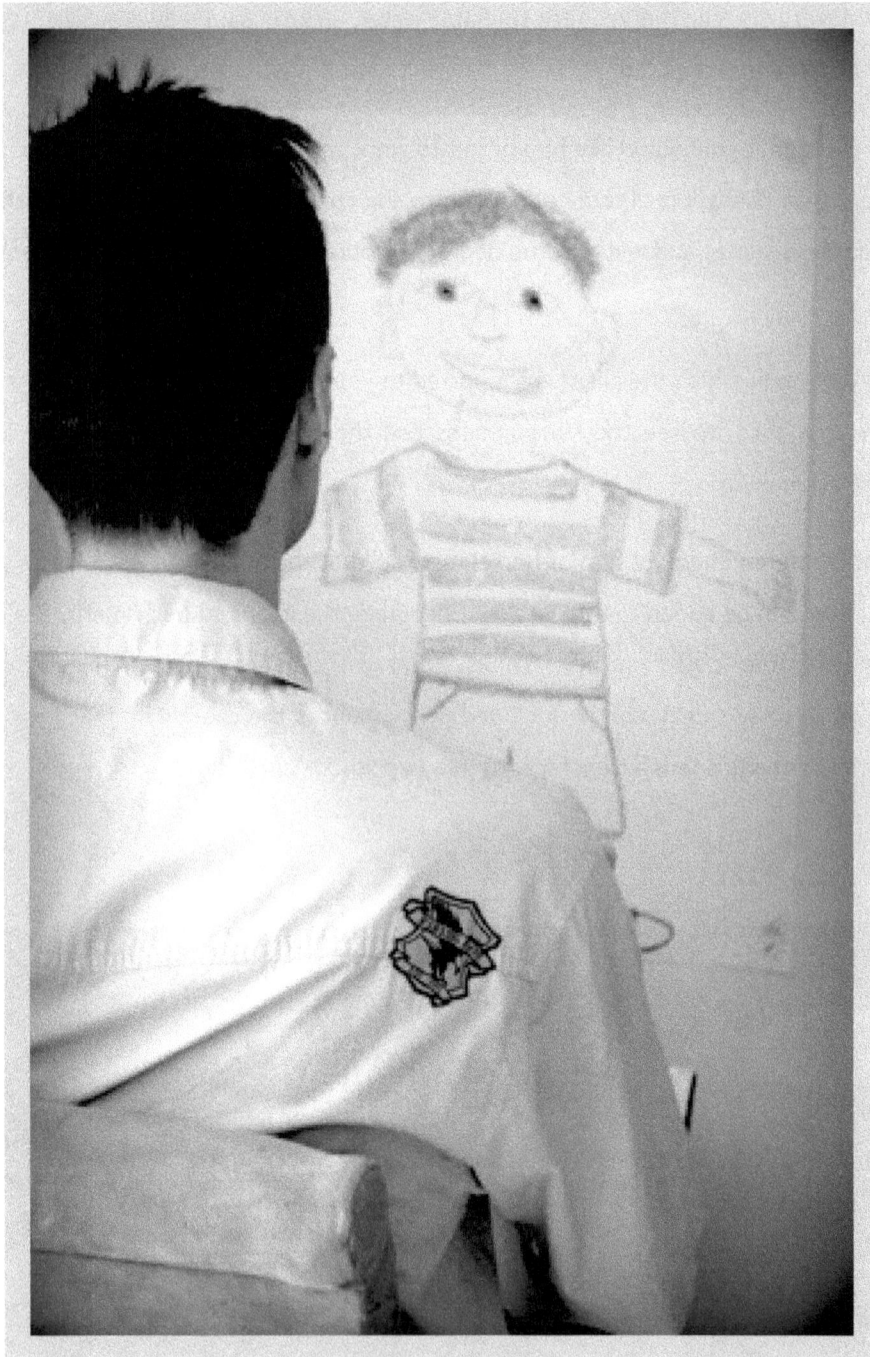

Allow plenty of time for the image to be quite detailed. Once complete, offer the client a chair to sit, and be sure that they are at eye level with the child's face. Give the client writing paper and several sharpened pencils. Instruct the client that the child-self will write with the non-dominant hand and the adult-self with the dominant hand. Begin to ask the client to address questions that you have previously constructed in line with the goals of therapy.

# CASE STUDY SIX

| | |
|---|---|
| **GOAL for therapy:** | *Resolving a woman's persistent rumination over her parent's divorce when she was only 6 years old. The goal for the inner child session is to reassure the child within that she is safe, and will be happy again in the future. Age of Child: 4* |

| | |
|---|---|
| **Therapist:** | Bella looks very happy here. I wonder if this is right? Can you ask her how she is feeling? Write this answer down. |
| **Adult Bella:** | Are you happy little Bella? |
| **Child Bella:** | Mmm sometimes. I like it when mummy plays with me. |
| **Therapist:** | Perhaps you can ask her more? Just keep going back and forth talking to her. When you are ready, I can help you with another question. |
| **Adult Bella:** | When are you not happy? |
| **Child Bella:** | When mummy and daddy are yelling it makes me sad. |
| **Bella:** | (addressing Therapist) What do I say now? |
| **Therapist:** | Is there some reassurance you can give her? |
| **Adult Bella:** | You know Mummy and Daddy love you even though they get cranky. It's not you they are angry with. |
| **Child Bella:** | I just want them to stop. I'm frightened. |
| **Adult Bella:** | You know, you are going to be all right. Mum and Dad are going to sort things out, and even though it won't be just what you want, you'll be ok. In fact sometimes it will be fun. And one day you will be grown up and then you'll be able to make your own life what you want. |
| **Child Bella:** | I don't think mummy and daddy love me anymore. I feel naughty. Like I've done something bad. I want to say sorry and make it better. |
| **Adult Bella:** | Well, they are so busy being angry at each other that they haven't got time for you. You have not done anything bad. It is mum and dad who are being naughty, not looking after you as well as they should. I want to give you a hug, make it all better. You don't deserve this. (Pause) You'll be ok. You will, I promise. |
| **Bella:** | (addressing the therapist) I'm not sure what else to say. |
| **Therapist:** | If Bella could ask you something about who you are now, what do you think she'd ask? |
| **Child Bella:** | Why are you always so sad? |

| Adult Bella: | I'm not sure. I feel like I've missed out on something. I feel like if I could just have done something, I might have stopped this from happening. I want Mum and Dad at my wedding but thinking about them being there makes me sad. Maybe I could do something to get them to make peace with each other. |
|---|---|
| Child Bella: | But you said it wasn't me doing anything wrong. How can you make it better? If Mummy and Daddy are sad, does that mean we have to be sad? |

(The session continues...)

The therapist in this circumstance may ask one or more of the following questions:

- What does the child Bella need to know to get through the next few years?
- What advice can you give the child Bella about her future?
- What do you think the child Bella might notice about you now?
- What assurances can you give to the child Bella about the future?

This process is best ended with the client making a commitment to the child. Encouraging the client to create or buy an object to gift to her inner child is useful, and a statement, to read aloud, honouring the child, will facilitate greater connection to and responsibility for the child within.

This work is best for adults. Some older teens may also respond well, but care needs to be taken to ensure that they have the maturity to demonstrate unconditional positive regard for themselves without ego/shadow interference.

Using sculpture or clay work to create a bust of the inner child or young adult, after the client has made peace with him or herself, can also be a powerful act.

*White air-dry clay, by Sophie Needs*

Experiential task

Consider a time in your childhood that precedes a difficult event. Following the inner child protocol outlined in this chapter, create the artwork, and the dialogue with dominant and non-dominant hands, to explore and honour the innocence of the child within at this point.

How has this activity facilitated integration of the child's voice in your life?

**Further reading**

Lucia Capaccione, *Recovery of Your Inner Child: The Highly Acclaimed Method for Liberating Your Inner Self*, Touchstone 1991

Cathryn L Taylor, *The Inner Child Workbook: What to do with your past when it just won't go away*, Tarcher 1991

# Meditation, relaxation, and guided imagery

Meditation has undergone a significant amount of study in recent years with research demonstrating the benefits that proponents have long argued for. Actual changes in the brain structure can be seen and these changes have implications for concentration, relaxation, mood regulation and impulse control (Holzel, Lazar, Gard, Schuman-Olivier, Vago, & Otto, 2011).

Studies have also shown that meditation increases gray matter in specific regions of the brain, increases cortical thickness and may slow the deterioration of the brain as a part of the natural aging process. (Lazar, et al., 2005)

It is clear that we do not only have access to our ordinary daily-wakened state or a sleep state to gather resources for healing. How we perceive a problem can vary significantly according to our 'state of mind' at the time. Taking the wrong turn in the car on a relaxed day may elicit very little self-criticism, but on a bad day may cause great self condemnation and even tears. Often a problem is finally resolved in that early morning twilight sleep, where the dreamer has one foot in the temporal world and another in a world devoid of time and limitations. Thus in this state, alternative realities are not just a possibility but a feature of twilight sleep. Capturing these moments to use intentionally can be remarkably fruitful.

Various states of meditation and active visualisation can allow the client to access possibilities previously unavailable. Freud in his model of therapy, sought to make the unconscious, conscious.

"The conscious mind may be compared to a fountain playing in the sun and falling back into the great subterranean pool of subconscious from which it rises." (Freud, 2010)

Jung asks us to connect to the collective unconscious, to examine symbols and archetypes as a way of understanding the human condition, and to see the truth about life that lies in the rhizome:

"Life has always seemed to me like a plant that lives on its rhizome. Its true life is invisible, hidden in the rhizome. The part that appears above ground lasts only a single summer. What we see is the blossom, which passes. The rhizome remains." (Jung, Memories, Dreams, Reflections Jung's autobiography, 1963)

If accessing other states of consciousness, and accessing unconscious material is so valuable, how do we make this happen? When we attempt to describe something we have perhaps not had to find words for before, we often look up, and spend a moment thinking, not usually because we don't know what we are about to reveal to another, but because we haven't found the best set of words yet to describe it. In seeking to communicate something we must reduce it to a set of symbols, albeit worded symbols, in order for this information to make sense to the listener. This process seldom fully captures what we wish to convey. It is a reductive process, and reduces our lived experience in its fullness, to a few select words, assessed as a best match for the listener's symbolic set. How we select the words depends also upon the listener. Trying to explain to an adult our sense of pointlessness is difficult, but conveying this to a child with a much more limited set of symbols would be quite problematic.

If words are reductive and conscious, a cognitive act of perception, memory, judgement, or reasoning, then a suspension of meaning making through words may make way for more unconscious material to present.

One method of accessing free associated material seems to be through meditation and guided visualisation. The therapist can assist the client to enter into this subtly altered state and facilitate the exploration using free association and allowing whatever comes to mind to be witnessed. This is not unlike what might occur in a dream state.

Despite our propensity to wonder about the nonsensical nature of our dreams, they are of our own making. Freud stated

"Obviously one must hold oneself responsible for the evil impulses of one's dreams. In what other way can one deal with them? Unless the content of the dream rightly understood is inspired by alien spirits, it is part of my own being." (Freud, 2010)

If this material is available in our minds, and so often has content relevant to our ordinary life, then accessing the unconscious may be about gaining access to such material in a wakened state. Although the monsters are not likely to appear in a wakened state, the feeling aroused may be evidence of an anxiety or fear that is yet unresolved.

Accessing unconscious material through Art Therapy is possible because the normal conscious cognitive processes are somewhat suppressed as the client enters the symbolic realm. This is especially possible if the client and the therapist utilise meditation and guided visualisation and enter into dialogue previously not used for the circumstance being addressed. If the client and therapist maintain an externalised dialogue, and one rich with the colours and shapes on the page, and make the known, somewhat unknown, it is as if the approach to the problem is in camouflage and the unconscious does not recognise the encroaching surveillance. As soon as the dialogue shifts back to meaning making or discussion of the problem, the unconscious is alerted. Once the unconscious is aware of the possible breach, it can quickly resort to well-rehearsed psychic defences, entering into battle and utilising the standard blocking approaches to keep the potentially unhelpful patterns in place.

Verbal therapies have no option but to approach an issue with dialogue.  Art Therapy can allow a very gentle approach that bypasses the standard worded descriptions that the client has possibly used many times before.  This alone can bring new insight; however making room for the unknown or indescribable to appear can add rich material for exploration and healing. Accessing other states of consciousness through relaxation, meditation, or guided visualisation can give access to internal resources previously unexplored.

Experiential task

The best way to learn about leading others in mediation and guided visualisation is to participate yourself in such activities.  Many digital media sources provide excellent guided meditations and visualisation that are inexpensive. Scripts for these are also available on the internet. When you have listened to a few, and enjoyed the benefits yourself, practice a gentle guided visualisation with a friend who will provide you with supportive, but critical feedback.

## Further Reading

Maureen Murdock, *Spinning Inward: Using Guided Imagery with Children for Learning, Creativity & Relaxation*, 1987, Shambhala

David Shannahoff Khalsa,  *Kundalini Yoga Meditation: Techniques Specific for Psychiatric Disorders, Couples Therapy, and Personal Growth*, 2007, W.W. Norton and Co.

Gillie Bolton (Ed), *Dying, Bereavement, and the Healing Arts*, 2007, Jessica Kingsley Publishers

# Dream Work

*"I have no theory about dreams, I do not know how dreams arise. And I am not at all sure that - my way of handling dreams even deserves the name of a "method." I share all your prejudices against dream-interpretation as the quintessence of uncertainty and arbitrariness. On the other hand, I know that if we meditate on a dream sufficiently long and thoroughly, if we carry it around with us and turn it over and over, something almost always comes of it. This something is not of course a scientific result to be boasted about or rationalized; but it is an important practical hint, which shows the patient, what the unconscious is aiming at. Indeed, it ought not to matter to me whether the result of my musings on the dream is scientifically verifiable or tenable; otherwise I am pursuing an ulterior - and therefore autoerotic - aim. I must content myself wholly with the fact that the result means something to the patient and sets his life in motion again. I may allow myself only one criterion for the result of my labours: does it work? As for my scientific hobby - my desire to know why it works - this I must reserve for my spare time." (Jung C. , 1931)*

Dreams lend themselves beautifully to Art Therapy processes. Once we fully accept that a dream is of our own making, then we can find value in examining how it came to be. Whether the dream is a divine intervention, a message from the cosmos or an invention of an overactive imagination is irrelevant in this approach. A dream has taken just some of the millions of possible storylines floating around in our unconscious, connected the dots (perhaps in a very haphazard way) and created a story. It's our story. We authored it ourselves. There may not be a predetermined meaning for this dream, but our efforts to understand it will be insightful. Just what we believe the feather boa wearing elephant to represent in our lives will say something about you and your world. And it will probably be different to someone else. Freud and Jung certainly postulated many sexual and archetypal meanings for the material in our dreams. (Freud, 2010) (Jung C. J., 1974) We may or may not find this information useful, but the searching will be.

The testing of hypothesis: Could this feather boa wearing elephant's trunk have some sexual relevance according to Freud's theories? Does the elephant speak of some Indian mystical knowledge? Or perhaps the feathers are representative of a tribal headdress? Actually, watching a hilarious rendition of the song 'Ellie the Elephant' has probably gotten snagged in my dream state! A dream has a foot in both worlds and may well reflect some of the action of our day.

Freud believed in the latent content in our dreams as holding the underlying psychological message, usually regarding a repressed and unfulfilled infantile sexual wish. Jung's position is that dreams create a balance between the good and the bad, the unconscious and conscious life, and thus could also account for the manifest content – that which is overt and is remembered. In a very simplified example, a person generally leading a mostly stress and anger free life, may have a frightful dream including an angry elephant in a feather boa, as a means of compensating or simply experiencing those somewhat foreign emotions (Jung C. J., 1974). This fits beautifully with Jung's eastern models of philosophy and the balance in all things.

Fritz Perls presented his theory of dreams as part of the holistic nature of Gestalt therapy. He suggested that dreams are projections of parts of the self that have been ignored, rejected, or suppressed. (Wegner, 2004) He argued that even inanimate objects in the dream can represent aspects of the dreamer.

Some cultures practised dream incubation with the intention of cultivating dreams that are prophetic (Lewis, 1994). A contemporary example can be incorporated in an art therapy model by ritualising an incubation of images created for example, about a repeatedly disturbing dream. The incubated dream can be allowed to sit for a session or two. After this period a ritual treatment of the incubated dream, and further art making may provide some insight, create meaning, or allow for some resolution or easing of the troublesome dream.

*A torn image of a dream in a mortar ready for the addition of other symbolic material to be ground and 'incubated' as a ritual act in uncovering the meaning of a dream.*

Recalling dreams can be a challenge. Regularly recording the dreams as you remember them can help. It is important to keep the dream journal by the bed. Brain chemicals necessary for converting experiences into long-term memory are suppressed during sleep, and thus remembering a dream experienced in the depth of the night is difficult. What often occurs is that a person will awaken during a dream, and as the experience is still very fresh, and in the short-term memory stores, it will only be remembered for a minute or two. Unless at this point the dreamer pays specific attention to recalling the detail in the dream, thus giving access to the neuro-chemicals generated whilst awake to activate long-term memory, the dream will be forgotten (Hobson & McCarly, 1977).

Engaging art in the exploration of dreams can be facilitated in many ways. A client can draw or paint the significant images and scenes from a dream. Often the client will report that they do not have enough clarity or detail. In this instance, reassure the client that the dream came from within, and that allowing intuition to guide them in creating detail will perhaps access the same unconscious material that originally generated the dream. Remember to again make the images that result, subject to a phenomenological investigation. Make the art unknown, perhaps by rotation or distance, and ask the client, "What do you see now?" "What does this mean to you?" "Does this have some relevance in (the goal for therapy generally or this activity)?" "What feelings are generated when you view this image?" (Note the continued externalisation by not asking the client what his or her feelings are.) Another useful exploration is to create the before and after images of a dream scene.

Encourage the client to identify objects in the dream, and explain them. What do they mean or represent? How might this object represent part of themselves or experience?

Ask the dreamer to imagine him or herself as any object or character within the dream. What feelings are generated? What resonance does the client feel with the object or character portrayed? What dissonance does the client experience? Where are the feelings of power and powerlessness?

Have the client create an answer to the questions posed by the dream. For example, the client may decide that the question posed is "What big elephant experience or belief am I inclined to dress up or enhance by adding a feather boa?" and "If the elephant is angry, is this exaggerating approach that I take going to blow up in my face?" The client can draw a single dream scene in answer, or perhaps a sequence.

Experiential task

Use your notebook by your bed to record any dreams you have over the next few weeks. Once you have a selection to choose from, create an art representation of the pivotal scene in each dream. Note the recurring themes in the dreams and the art. Consider these in light of Freud and Jung's approach to dream interpretation.

**Further Reading**

Arthur Freeman, *Cognitive Therapy and Dreams*, 2003, Springer

James A Hall, *Jungian Dream Interpretation: A Handbook of Theory and Practice*, 1983, Inner City Books

# Life and Death Drives

Just as many contemporary psychological models can be incorporated into an Art Therapy practice, so too can traditional models of psychoanalysis. Many concepts, particularly those of Freud and Jung, can be adapted to provide useful explorations for clients.

Life and death drives as initially described by Freud can be valuable concepts to explore, particularly for expressions of depression and dissatisfaction. It is the tension between the two realms that is challenging for many, yet so necessary.

Creating art that speaks of the darkness, or the many small and real deaths and endings, can seem like a morbid pursuit. Many deeply depressed or disturbed people engage voluntarily in such art work as a means of expressing the depths of despair, or as a means of purging. Alone such art work may indicate an urgent need for greater support, but within the framework of therapy, explorations of death can be surprisingly life affirming.

A client may create the 'full extent of the darkness' in an image, depicting the little deaths, the endings, the potentials unfulfilled, the fears, the unknown, the pain, sadness and chaos, or the simple nothingness of death.

The second image would be of the life drive, Eros, dancing in the sun, creativity, possibility, life, renewal, births, beginnings and joy.

It is important that the client is supported to become aware of the necessity of death to provide an impetus for life. The client may need to develop some acceptance of the permanence of the darkness's presence. This is often a causal factor in depression and dissatisfaction and a tolerance of the darkness is essential to healing.

Once complete the client can place both art pieces somewhere in the room, relevant to his or her experience of the life and death drives in his or her life. The therapist can then ask, "Where are you standing between these two places now?" The client can try positions, moving around until he or she is satisfied. The therapist may ask "So when you are in this position in life, like now, which direction do you face?" This is not unlike the half-full or half-empty glass question. The therapist asks, "Do you look toward the sadness, or the joy, or do you ignore both?" These explorations can be further extended to enquire what position the client would like to take given that perhaps he or she is currently unable to change the position on the life/death drive spectrum. What might it take for the client to turn around, or even to take a step in one direction or another?  What is the image that best represents the position in which he or she currently stands? How does the image look in the place he or she wishes to be?

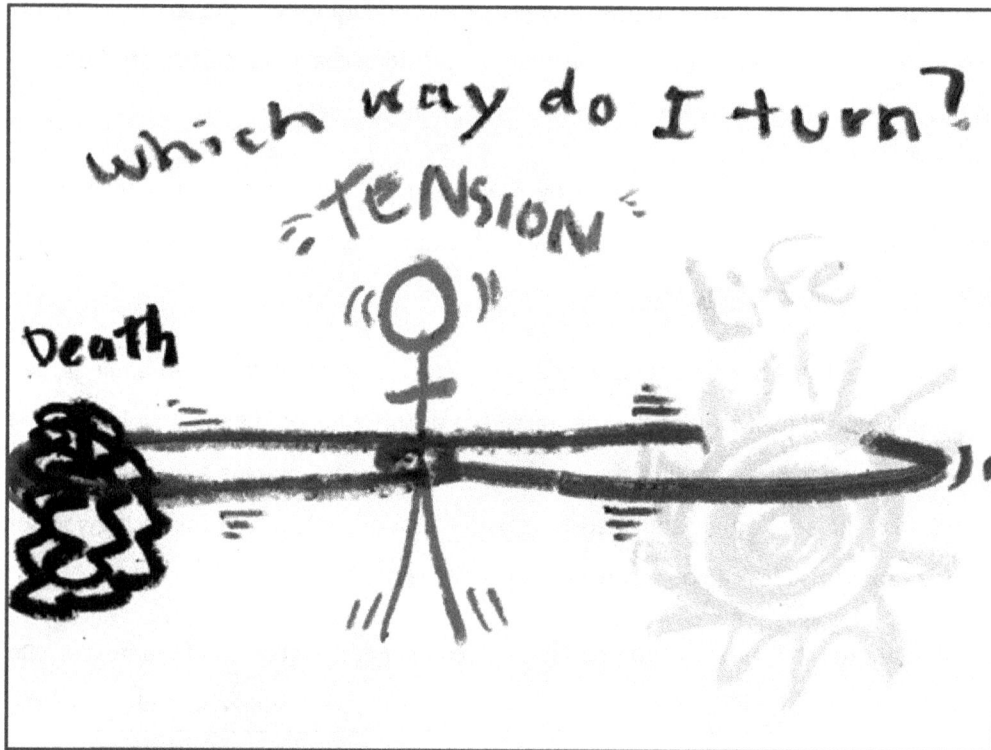

Experiential task

Imagine yourself with 2 elastic bands around your waist, one has a gentle but constant pull toward death, another the gentle but constant pull to life.  Recall a time where the pull of one, and the denial of the other were strongest.  Draw this representation and be sure you are in the image. Where are you standing? What are you facing?  What elements are increasing the pull?

As this is an activity not designed to provide resolution of any kind, be sure to finish with an activity or ritual that aids closure for this exploration.

**Further Reading**

Ernest Beck, *The Denial of Death*, 1997, Free Press

# Mandala

One of the most common assumptions I hear people make about Art Therapy is that it is all about mandala drawing!  This art process is indeed valuable, but no more or less than many others.

It does however; provide a simple activity that requires little preparation or materials. This makes it a good mobile therapist's activity. Another very simple, portable and no-fail activity with similar attributes is the Zentangle.  Rick Roberts and Maria Thomas created the Zentangle art form and method.  This simple art process can be used wherever you might work with Mandala. You can find out more about Zentangles by visiting www.zentangle.com

Mandala is a Sanskrit word meaning "circle". Many followers of the Hindu and Buddhist traditions use mandala as a mediation tool.   The traditional shape is a square overlaid with a circle.  The art evolves from a central point. These concentric diagrams have spiritual and ritual significance. The Tibetan monks also create sand mandala. Once completed the designs are then poured back in a creek or riverbed. This act parallels the Art Therapist's stance of generally valuing the process over the product.  Carl Jung saw the mandala as a representation of the unconscious self, a medium through which he could identify his own emotion ailments and an activity through which he could heal.

Mandala can be created with specific intent in relation to the client's goal, or as an incidental therapeutic activity, whilst developing a relationship with the client, or when establishing groups.

**For a directed activity:**

Frame the question: What do you wish for the mandala to reveal?  Explain that the mandala will be finished today, but the revelation may come slowly over a few hours, days or weeks.

Begin with a guided meditation and visualisation.  Encourage the client to trust his or her inner wisdom to bring colours, shapes and lines as keys to the revelation. Once the client is ready to begin, ask him or her to take a deep breath and to clear the minds of thoughts and worries. Ask the client to just allow him or herself to be drawn to a colour, and to just begin with whatever line or shape comes to them.  The image will ideally unfold without conscious mental direction. There is no right or wrong.   Once the image is complete, ask the client to give it a title.

Many approaches can now be used with this resulting product. Rotation of the image, looking at it from afar and in a different light may reveal some interesting details relevant to the client's goal. The client may dialogue with the image, asking direct questions of the mandala and answering through additional art pieces or with words. A more interpretative approach may be used, where the client seeks to find a personal meaning for the shapes, colours and lines. The mandala may be placed where the client will see it often and can be prepared to await an intuitive message from the art.

Mandala can be used with groups in many interesting ways. If the group members are previously unknown to one another, a mandala of shared and unique experiences will assist in bonding the group, sharing stories and will give the facilitator time to observe the group dynamic in preparation for perhaps more challenging work for the participants. For example, a group established for the support of newly bereaved parents may complete a mandala in the first few sessions, or indeed as the entire series of sessions. After an introduction the participants would be asked to create a single large mandala with representations of those experiences that they have all experienced throughout their journey to bereavement, placed in the centre of the circle. At the edges of the circle, participants are asked to represent the experiences that have been unique to their journey. Thus the participants will be discussing experiences and determining if these are shared or unique.

As a result, two distinct outcomes occur. Parents share, they disclose information and support one another in doing so. This can create a tremendous bond, and establish a support network without overtly setting this up. The second outcome is participants discover that they are not so alone as they first believed. Parents inevitably discover that many others have experienced similar situations and circumstances. The shared centre of the art is usually much larger than first assumed. The mandala may then be photographed and made into postcards, or framed. Finally, the group can decide on a ritual parting with the art work. Would the group members like to cut the mandala up and each keep small pieces? Would the participants like to ritualistically burn it, freeing it to the earth? Would they like to roll it up and each keep it for a time, with a handover occurring at a monthly coffee meeting? The ritual of closure can be an important element of the therapy.

Mandala 'blanks', small cards with a pre drawn circle, left in a waiting room along with some felt tip markers or coloured pencils, can be a great anxiety reliever. In my consulting studio I have an area of wall where clients and other visitors can stick a Velcro sticky spot to the back of the completed mandala and attach it to a carpeted piece of wall. This art, as it is not created within the therapy session itself, is quite reasonable to display. The choice remains with the creator as he or she can remove the art if, and when, they choose. The wall is a growing, ever changing art piece, a quilt of creative moments. Even my postman has completed one!

Experiential task

Create an 'opening' mandala. Imagine this as the key to being open to new ideas, learning and opportunities. Incorporate meditation and allow your unconscious to guide the process with limited thinking about how to structure this design.

## Further reading

Bailey Cunningham, *Mandala: Journey to the Center*, 2003, DK Adult

C. G Jung, *Mandala Symbolism (Bollingen Series)*, 1976, Princeton University

# Story and Art Therapy

So often the use of an externalised model of therapy, the construction of metaphor and the freedom to create, results in a great deal of storytelling. This often occurs naturally throughout the therapy sessions and noting details of the story may make it possible to construct an actual storybook as a celebration of the journey taken, the results achieved, or the hurdles overcome. A method for such storytelling that has become increasingly popular in psychotherapy in recent years is the Hero's Journey.

This concept was documented and explored by anthropologists and mythologists such as Otto Rank (1922) and Joseph Campbell in The Hero with a Thousand Faces (1949) who more extensively described the stages and universality of this model. A wonderful feminine version of the concept of the everyday hero is The Heroine's Journey by Maureen Murdock (1990).

This monomyth, as it is often referred to, is a universal story structure now used by writers and filmmakers the world over. Not only does the model beautifully encapsulate the cyclic calls to adventure, the struggles, battles, desperation, successes and personal growth, but the structure of such stories has great appeal to humankind. Our experience in battling with an old washing machine has parallels with Luke Skywalker's struggles in Star Wars. We might not have such huge life and death issues to deal with on a daily basis, but for many people the supposedly small battles can be, at times, overwhelmingly big. It is our empathy for the character in the story that generates a sense of resonance and this resonance connects human beings.

Story telling in therapy not only further enables externalisation, metaphoric expression and presentation of unconscious material, but it also allows the story teller the power to connect with the listener, the audience. The old English proverb, 'a troubled shared is a trouble halved' somehow resonates with this ability we have to leave some of our pain with another in the form of empathy. Even in celebration, we join together, advertise our success and take great joy from the ability of others to 'feel' our joy.

Thus a story telling and art based book making process can be extremely beneficial in therapy. The book itself memorialises the experience, the challenges, the battles and the joys. It is a trophy and a reminder of the journey - The Hero's Journey!

The model used in therapy is now quite diverse but maintains the same basic stages as was first recorded by Joseph Campbell. The following outline is a modified version that can be used in therapeutic storytelling.

*The Ordinary World*

What is the ordinary, everyday world in which this hero lives? Perhaps it is a naive existence, or perhaps a self centred one. Or perhaps it is full of innocence and joy. This first stage sets the scene. It is the 'before' picture.

*The Journey's Call*

This is the point in a person's life when the circumstances first align for change. The Hero may or may not be aware of this impending change.

*Refusal of the Call*

The call may not be welcome. The would-be Hero may be afraid or resentful. There may be many circumstances that make the impending adventure less than desirable. A delay may occur here.

*The Helper appears*

Once the hero has engaged, consciously or unconsciously, the helper appears. This is often in the form of a person but may also be an idea, a philosophy, or some other support.

*Crossing of the Threshold*

Here is where the journey begins. It is the point where the hero moves away from the familiar and into the unknown. It is often frightening and dangerous, although a little naiveté here is not uncommon either.

*The In-Between World*

This is the place where there is no longer a connection to the old world, but the new world is still a mystery. It is not necessarily the lowest point in the journey, but it is certainly the loneliest. The stepping into the in-between world is where the hero makes a commitment to the journey ahead.

*The Challenges*

In this stage, the Hero must begin the work of transformation of becoming the Hero - overcoming trials and tribulations to keep battling on forward. In modern screenwriting these trials are usually numerous. Many times the Hero will fail only to learn something invaluable to take into the next battle.

*The Meeting with the Inner Divine*

Here the Hero meets his or her own divinity or god-likeness. This meeting is allows the Hero to feel absolute love, and acceptance for him or herself, for others, and for the greater good. It can be about putting one's own needs aside.

Philosopher Jeremy Bentham in 1776 believed, "it is the greatest happiness of the greatest number that is the measure of right and wrong" (Bentham & Harrison, 1988) Spock, a Vulcan of Star Trek fame, sacrificed his own life for others stating, "The needs of the many outweigh the needs of the few, or of the one". This is often the stage of the journey where the individual matters less than the outcome or the principle. In love stories it is that point of surrendering oneself to another. In an action movie it is a preparedness to risk life and limb to fight for the cause. In a drama it is often the point of complete healthy self-love and acceptance.

*The Temptations*

Often at some point in the Hero's journey, temptations arise. This may be in the form of an encounter with someone, something or some part of one's own shadows in the psyche. It may be the time of engaging false promises and false hope. This stage is often tinged with repulsion at the weaknesses within oneself.

*The Critical Event*

The Critical Event occurs when the temptations have passed, when the road ahead is obvious and there is clearly no going back. It is a confrontation with the inevitable or the ultimate power. This is the centre of the journey. The Hero knows that life can never be the same. The Hero will never be the same. It is as Freud would say "A little death". In many stories actual death can be recorded in this stage. Many families whose children have died will draw, paint or write about the moment of death in this stage. It is quite healing for those with a strong spiritual belief to see this moment as the beginning of a new way of being, and the moment of transformation in the relationship they have with the child. In grieving, we do not 'end' a relationship - we build a new one with the memories and values of the person lost to us, embedded in our own soul.

### The Veneration

When someone 'dies' to the old-self to live in new knowledge, he or she moves into a god-like state. If the person has a physical death he or she is in heaven and beyond all strife. A simpler way of looking at this step is that it is a period of self-honouring - a period of rest, peace and fulfilment before the Hero begins the return.

### The Boon

The boon is the achievement of the goal of the quest. It is what the person went on the journey to get. All the previous steps serve to prepare and purify the person for this step, since in many myths the boon is something transcendent like a spiritual experience, wisdom beyond words or the key to heaven.

### Trusting the Process

The Hero discovered guides and assistants when he or she set out on the journey. Even in the return, the Hero may need support in some form. Here the important message is about relinquishing all control and sometimes surrendering to others for support.

### Bearing Gifts

The Hero must retain the wisdom gained on the quest, and have the skills and resources to integrate that wisdom into an everyday human life. This alone, is not enough. The Hero must also bring something back in this journey for others.

### The New World

The Hero needs to understand where he came from and where he is now. It may mean achieving a balance between the material and spiritual. The Hero has perhaps become comfortable and competent in both the inner and outer worlds. This mastery leads to freedom from the fear of death, which in turn is the freedom to live. This is sometimes referred to as living in the moment, neither anticipating the future nor regretting the past, but just being.

The Hero's journey model can be constructed through an art process before the story itself is constructed. For instance, the client would be asked to identify a character, object, animal or symbol to represent themselves in the story. Let's imagine for a moment the client has stated they would like themselves to be a seagull. The first stage, the client may identify the seagull living a (lonely, connected, angry, desperate) life, and depict this metaphorically in the first image. In the second stage, The Call to Adventure, perhaps the client is exploring his or her move to a new continent, beginning a marriage, or finishing up with an employer. Perhaps the client will depict the seagull knowing of a supposedly amazing island, just slightly further away than any other seagull has flown, and being drawn to take the trip. In the stage where the Supernatural Aid appears, perhaps this is when the seagull meets an old pelican, who knows of another who made this trip. The client may recognise the inner wisdom, the voice of a trusted friend, or a newly gained qualification as keys to aiding his or her journey.

The important factor here is in maintaining the art before the dialogue. Just as with all Art Therapy the aim is not to predetermine the story with words, but to allow other possibility to emerge, to allow the unconscious the freedom to contribute.

Once all images are complete, the story writing process can occur. Ask the client to carefully view and review each art image for other insights about the journey prior to commencing the writing.

This Hero's journey process can be used to celebrate successful journeys, to reflect on a partial journey and find inspiration and motivation for the completion of it.

The Hero's journey can also be applied to death and dying. Despite our traditional notions of success not ending in death, those with strong spiritual beliefs can see death as the Hero's reward - but alas suffering for those left behind. In this instance a hero's journey can provide a spiritual bolster, memorialising the courageous life and final transcendence and can be completed by the individual or those who grieve or after his or her death. In memorialising a person who has died, the final destination may be signified as success if the person was able to make some lasting change in the world, or for the people who loved him or her.

After writing the story, the construction of a book - a unique, hand-bound volume perhaps made as part of the therapeutic work - can have immense value.

Many stories and movies have some therapeutic benefit and can open up dialogue that is less easily accessed from the position of the client. For instance discussing parenting matters from a relevant movie is often less confronting for a parent and may, in the early stages, facilitate the therapy.

*boUnd, 2011, Ky Alecto*

Experiential task

Identify a time in your life, where you had to be a 'hero' to navigate a particular journey. Use the model outlined in this chapter to create the images and then write your own "Hero's Journey".

How has your thinking changed about this situation since you have completed the Hero's journey task?

**Further Reading**

Garry Solomon, *Reel Therapy: How Movies Inspire You to Overcome Life's Problems*, 2001, Aslan Publishers

Ryan Niemiec and Danny Wedding, *Positive Psychology At The Movies: Using Films to Build Virtues and Character Strengths*, 2008, Hogrefe Publishing

Robert Atkinson *The Gift of Stories: Practical and Spiritual Applications of Autobiography, Life Stories, and Personal Mythmaking*, 1995, Bergin & Garvey Paperback

George W Burns, *101 Healing Stories: Using Metaphors in Therapy*, 2001, Wiley

# Ritual

Our daily lives are imbedded in ritual in ways we might not at first recognise. Certainly as a culture we have particular rituals. As individuals we have family rituals and possibly some acknowledged personal rituals. But the habitual component of living goes much further than this. Next time you shower, stop and observe how you do this daily 'ritual'. The chances are that you tend to do the same thing, over and over. Another method may be just as effective, but this one has become a habit. The hand that holds the soap or the shower gel, just how you twist your body, where you start and where you finish. The position you stand in the shower, the action of a round-and-round scrubbing motion or a smoothing and stroking. Then when you dry off, the ritual here otherwise known as a routine or habit is also well embedded. Even if we think we are pretty random and don't have a plan for showering and drying, one almost certainly has developed. And if you try to alter this, and do it differently, it all feels a little strange.

The definitions of ritual, routine and habit have some significant overlaps.

Ritual: an act done in accordance with social custom or normal protocol. A religious or solemn ceremony consisting of a series of actions performed according to a prescribed order.

Habit: a behaviour pattern acquired by frequent repetition or physiologic exposure that shows itself in regularity or increased facility of performance; an acquired mode of behaviour that has become nearly or completely involuntary.

Routine: a regular course of procedure, habitual or mechanical performance of an established procedure (Britannica)

It is clear that these three words have a great deal in common. Frequently, what begins as a routine may develop into a habit with a prescribed order, which can then become an almost sacred ritual. A ritual is hard to define as a single event, as it is usually performed as a culmination of events, or as a repetition. Occasionally a ritual is a single event in the performance, but even then is comprised of a preparation process and longevity of the act can be significant. A ritual is often imbued with great history, reverence and repetition, with a good dose of Jung's collective unconscious feeding into it. When studied as such, rituals are archetypal ideas in action. The wedding is a ritual worthy of its own full volume.

Neuroscience theories suggest that habit making, routines and rituals are part of the brain's self care mechanism. The suggestion is that in placing a set of actions or behaviours into the brain's 'automatic pilot', much less effort is required in 'thinking' and thus reserves the brain's energy for more immediate concerns. If we think about riding a bike as a habit, we can see that in the beginning the effort required in maintaining balance, steering, determining the bike's centre of gravity and so on is considerable. If we were asked to answer a difficult question at the same time as riding in the early days, we would almost certainly need to stop riding the bike to think clearly. Once competent however, we can ride the bike without thinking and thus use those reserves for other important matters, such as answering difficult questions.

In therapy it is common for a client's goal to contain elements of developing a new habit, of acting or being differently, where little or no effort is required once the skill is acquired. Where, for instance, maintaining appropriate boundaries can be the default position rather than an internal battle the client has to repeatedly navigate.

Ritual in therapy might best be defined as a structured set of actions developed collaboratively by the therapist and client to effect a transition from one psychological state to another. This transition may be a form of initiation, or it may be focused on intrapersonal or interpersonal change, such as releasing anger or resentment, or even self-criticism.

The ritual may be a one-time act, imbued with great meaning or a ritual can be used like a daily prayer, changing the patterning and restructuring the undesired behaviour at a neurological level (McMillan, 2005).

So how does ritual development in therapy lead to such habit changes? Rituals "remind us that communication can be symbolic, that form gives meaning, that repetition promotes learning and that the past is embedded in the present" (Bennett & Wolin, 1984). A ritual can provide emotional investment, reverence and an embodied process that can lead to a powerful new pattern. Rituals consist not only of the act, performance or ceremony itself, but the whole process of preparing for it, experiencing and reintegrating the experience and value back into the event and life. A ritual can powerfully reinforce itself. The client may spend two sessions planning, imagining and acting out the ritual movement required to step into the next era in his or her life. Anticipation adds weight to the psychological investment. A day and time is assigned as a turning point. The ritual is undertaken, the emotion is often high, thus adding to the honouring of the commitment, and creating a cycle of power. E.g. "My commitment is important, the act feels emotional and significant, thus my honouring it is important. This means that commitment is paramount, the act of staying true to it feels honest, thus my honouring it is important", and so on as the cycle continues. It is, as clearly stated by Bennett and Wolin, symbolic repetition promoting learning. A well planned and anticipated single ritual fully integrated in the therapy can create a loop of learning significant in creating longer-term outcomes for the client.

Two ways in which we can incorporate powerful rituals into an Art Therapy process are through establishing rituals for containment, at each end of a therapy session, and developing a ritual to mark a significant spiritual/psychological event.

For many clients, the introduction of a routine in engagement can be quite supportive. For instance, a client who is routinely asked to sit in the waiting room for 10 minutes before the session, and to focus on the trickling water fountain to allow the tensions and stressors of the week to wash away before the session begins, will look forward to this, and may in fact be quite unsettled to see the fountain is out of order! It is not that the fountain holds any magical power, but the ritual itself, the time set aside to free oneself from the tensions and stressors, is potent. The anticipation and expectation of what is to result from this action adds value to the effort. Similarly, when a session regularly ends with a short movement activity, the therapist can remind the client of his or her resilience and capacity for self-care, and that he or she can trust the body to lead him or her through the week ahead. By establishing a helpful ritual within the therapy, clients will often generalise these skills and develop or transfer rituals that support them in day to day living. The routine that you as the therapist might establish can become a habit for the client, and one can hope, eventually become a supportive ritual in his or her life.

Ritual can also act in marking a significant therapeutic event. This ritual is not an established pattern of behaviour, but the aim is for it to become a ritualistic action. For instance, a client may complete fifteen sessions of therapy and in the final session, ritualize the act of walking through the door into a world of diligent self-care. That action embodies the process - it gives the client a physical act, symbolic of the action required in self-care. It is hoped that the action acts upon the sensory system's memory in a way that causes a ritualistic or revered act of self-care.

Other significant psychological events may be ritualised in tearing or burning of art products, in boxing up or containing material. It may be in releasing the art materials back to the earth in the form of burying, or finely shredding and allowing the art to blow away in the wind. The presence of witnesses can add significance to ritualised verbal declarations and actions.

Experiential task

If you have read and completed each task up to this point, begin to plan a ritual for finishing the journey you have taken with me in "Art Therapy: Foundation and Form"

Prepare statements and actions that reinforce a commitment to move forward with the positive learning that has occurred, and to feel confident in your new knowledge. Prepare also to allow those approaches or statements that do not resonate with you, to wash off, and fall away, leaving just that which is beneficial.

Be sure to include materials you have generated during this journey in ways that support you in the ritual.

Plan to action this ritual on a particular day and time, when you know you will have finished the remaining few pages of this text.

**Further Reading**

Evan Imber-Black, Janine Roberts, Richard Alva Whiting, *Rituals in Families and Family Therapy*, 1988, W.W. Norton and Co.

Claire Schrader, *Ritual Theatre: The Power of Dramatic Ritual in Personal Development Groups and Clinical Practice*, 2011, Jessica Kingsley Publishers

# The Art Therapist's tool kit

There are no hard and fast rules about what items need to be in a portable Art Therapy kit. The most important consideration is in the choice of mediums. It is important to have mediums that will resonate with a variety of emotions and ways of being. Limiting your kit to a packet of pencils is not only limiting the qualities available for experience, but also limiting the clients whom you can support to those who have the capacity to hold and direct a pencil as they wish.

Mobile kits need to take into account the weight of materials, the ability to use materials in a variety of spaces and access to appropriate work spaces (e.g. something solid on which to mould air dry clays, or a stable, level surface for marbling work), the ability to use the mediums safely, (e.g. ventilation), and clean-up facilities, (e.g. sink, bins, towels for spills).

Good quality clay is preferable for a studio but white air-drying clay is easier for a portable kit. Clean up is a lot easier and there are no concerns about clogging pipes or staining carpets in other people homes or hospital rooms.

Marbling kits need careful consideration as oil-based products can have odours that impact on the therapy. Products that need considerable dry time are also much less suited to portable work. Fixative for soft pastel work is not advised for use with or around clients. This would be reasonable if the client chooses to use these products themselves, but such products can cause significant reactions in some people and should be used cautiously. Likewise, when working with clients who have physical illness, smells can be particularly offensive in some circumstances, particularly those undergoing chemotherapy.

# Basic Mobile Kit

Paper A3 80gsm plain paper

A4 quality cartridge paper

A4 thin cardboard

Assorted origami paper

Chalky soft pastels

Oil pastels

Watercolour pencils

Watercolour wheel and 4 brushes

Felt tip markers

Fine liners (fine tip markers)

Scissors

Cutting knife and board

Aluminium foil

Pencil sharpener

Glue stick

Masking tape

Ruler

Coloured pencils

Graphite pencils

Glue gun and glue sticks

Pop sticks

Crafting wire

Plastic cups

Sandwich bag of dry casting plaster

Lunch box of small craft objects, including
beads, sequins, nuts and bolts, feathers,

gumnuts, stones, shells, threads, strings and cottons

Marbling inks and tray (the lid of the box can sometimes be used for a tray)

White modelling air dry clay, plasticine or play-dough

Basic clay tools

Avocado stones

Lino carving tools

Blu-tac or similar

Rubber bands

Paper towel

Newspaper

Tissues and hand wipes

If space permits, a portable sand play kit

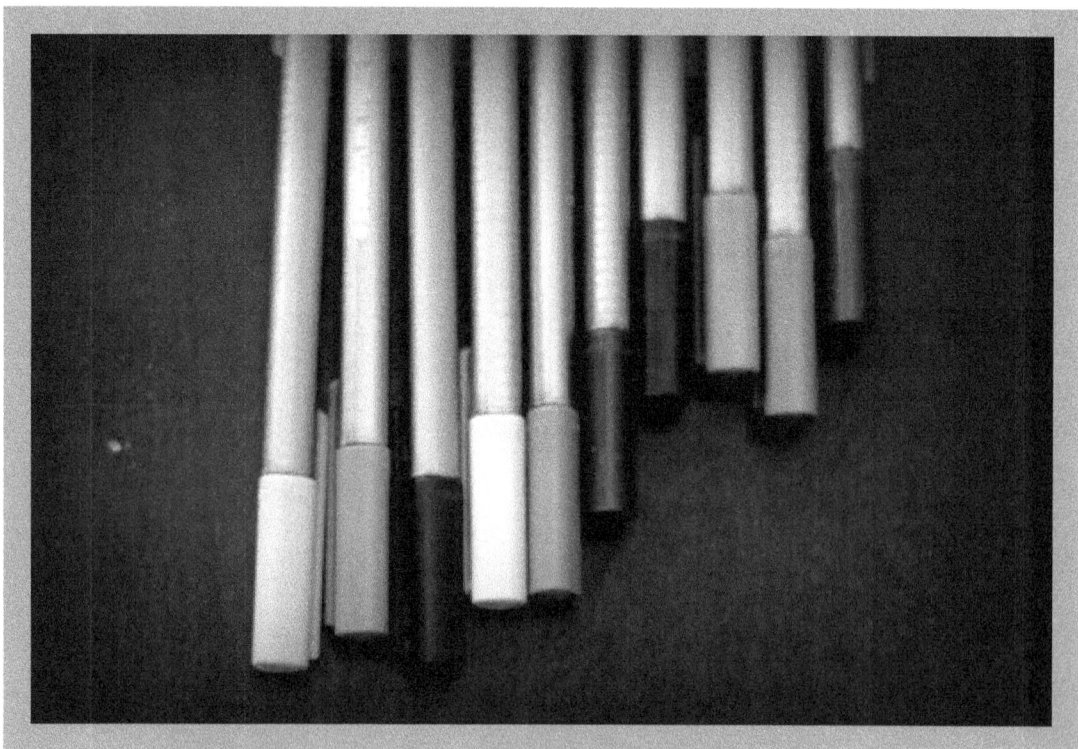

# Basic Studio Consulting Kit

All of the Basic Kit items, including sand play kit

**and**

Additional small objects for sand play work

Acrylic Paints

Assortment of brushes and sponges

Old magazines, pictures, wrapping papers for collage

Wallpaper glue

Mirror

Old telephone books

Clay and silt bucket

Sponges and clay tools

Small aerated concrete blocks  (approx. 20 cm x 20 cm x 20 cm)

Carving tools

Facemasks

Linoleum tiles for printmaking

Blender, frames and tubs for papermaking

Large construction wire and pliers

Rolls of brown paper

Scrap booking materials

Fabric scraps

Yourself!  - The final, but most important item for the Art Therapist's Tool Kit. The most valuable asset in your tool kit is you.  You will need to keep this in good condition, and subject it to regular scrutiny to ensure it does the job assigned and causes no damage.

# The Art of Self-Care and Reflection

As a human services professional, one of the most critical elements in maintaining a passion for what I do is carefully managing boundaries and self-care. This means keeping a balance between my professional and personal lives, looking at how my body and mind are responding to the way I live, and sometimes being prepared to say "No" even when I want to say "Yes". The quickest way to burn out in your chosen profession is to ignore the warning signs and battle on despite them. I often find myself using art as a means of reflecting not just on my day or the issues that a client might bring to therapy, but to further observe and understand my way of being in the world. I use the art to tell a story. I look to art for insight and guidance. I pay attention to what comes up for me and, finally, I act upon this new knowledge. Try it for yourself.

Imagine an old castle, a stronghold, a place that metaphorically holds your professional practice. In order to maintain your ability to keep doing this work, you need to protect the castle. The drawbridge is often down and all the townsfolk can come to the castle for whatever they may need and, in fact, many may also bring elements that enrich your practice.

Imagine your passion for your role as a fire burning brightly in the middle of this castle. Imagine that the timbers that feed the fire and keep the castle warm are the symbols of a sense of achievement. They may be the successes, big and small, that you might experience each day. These logs are the energy stores that help keep this fire burning and the fuel you use to continue the work you do.

Some days, the fire might burn low and the logs to feed the fire may be few. Perhaps on these days you spend time talking to a good friend, a colleague or a supervisor and you are reminded of what you bring to the lives of others. These people will hand you another log for the fire to restore the passion and have the fire burn brightly again.

Around the castle is a moat. The moat is a special space - a sacred space. This is the area that you expect people to respect. In a good, strong castle's moat, swim creatures wonderful to behold, but unwise to swim with. Anyone who seeks to gain access to your practice by unfair or deceptive means climbs into your moat. This might be the client who follows you home, or seeks you out through means other than agreed upon by the terms of your engagement. Do you, on occasion allow someone to swim in the moat? Do you allow a more intimate relationship to develop to foster a therapeutic alliance? What are the risks of allowing someone to swim in the moat?

Sometimes without appropriate protection in the moat, someone will sneak into the castle. This can be frightening, and a real threat to your capacity to keep the castle's fire burning. Be sure you have determined who is swimming in the moat as protection. Is it your boss? Perhaps you also have the police?

To provide your clients with a service they must come to the castle's drawbridge. The door guards lower the drawbridge and when the work is done, draw it up tight. Perhaps they have instructions to lower the drawbridge on weekdays and raise it on the weekend. Perhaps there are some conditions where the guards may choose to lower the drawbridge. Perhaps a client is in immediate need. Will you answer a phone call from a client at 11 pm? To imply that he or she cannot manage without you indicates an unequal power, a relationship of neediness rather than self-empowerment. So will you lower the drawbridge? Perhaps it is during your daughter's birthday party. Do you potentially hurt those closest to you to support another? Perhaps you have worked seven days straight and are exhausted. Do you risk your own wellbeing for that of a client? Does this model an appropriate way of being? Be sure your door guards know the answers to these questions and clearly know when it is appropriate to lower the drawbridge and when the castle needs to be locked tight.

Just inside the heavy doors of this castle is a large mirror. This mirror is a truth teller - like the mirror in Snow White, it must be honest with the reflection. What do you see? How well do you know yourself? Can you look yourself in the eye when you are about to embark upon an action that is not true to yourself or respecting of reasonable, healthy boundaries and self care?

Who stands at the battlements on the very top of the castle overlooking your practice? This may well be a professional accrediting body, your clinical supervisor, or even your boss at work. You will also have the law keeping an eagle eye on your practice. It might be worthwhile to place your partner or a trusted friend here also. This can be the person who asks "Is this the third night out this week for work?" or "I can see you are not coping so well at the moment, what about a few days off?" This person may also say, "This is great. I don't know the inner workings of the castle, but from here I can feel the warmth from the fires inside and I can see how happy people are when they leave here".

This castle metaphor also gives us an opportunity to reflect upon transference and counter-transference that may interfere in the therapeutic relationship.

Attached to the castle is a tower where a 'princess' resides. This princess wants to be rescued. Perhaps she is afraid and in need of a big strong person in her life, when just such a client appears on the drawbridge. Can you hear the princess calling out? Perhaps she is crying, "Oh, let him in. It'll be ok." Many women have spoken to me about how the princess in them cries out when they are treated especially well by a client. Can you see how perhaps she is seeking some balm for her sense of poor treatment in her own life? When might a client activate the 'princess' in you that needs rescuing?

The dungeon is where the prisoner is locked away. The prisoner is inclined to rattle the chains, bang on the door and become aggressive when a client activates him. Many people, when they first hear of a client committing an abusive act, can feel the prisoner trying to escape. This prisoner would love to get out on the drawbridge and teach this client a thing or two, usually with some physical aggression. Perhaps the client taps into some unresolved sense of injustice in your own life, and the prisoner fires up. When might a client uncover something deep and repressed?

During those times where great love and admiration, or deep anger and resentment surface, ask yourself, is the 'princess' crying out, are you in need of something the client offers, or is the prisoner wanting to save someone, somewhere in time, or wanting to set things straight?

I know often that when things get a little 'wobbly' in a therapeutic relationship, that I will frequently explore with my supervisor a sense of a 'crying princess' or 'rattling chains'.

Spend some time drawing your castle on a large piece of paper. Use the metaphor in as many ways as is applicable to your practice. Then stand back and look. What do you see? What can you learn about yourself and how you operate in your profession that will help you keep the fires burning and the passion for your profession bright?

Self-care is not just for us. If we do not care for our own wellbeing, we model inappropriate self-care to our clients and ultimately without this awareness, we will burn out and be unable to do this valuable work at all. Stop and take measure often, and keep those fires burning brightly!

# Conclusion

Art Therapy is not a fixed science; rather it is an evolving one. Not only is the breadth of Art Therapy practice as a profession changing, but also it is where the individual practitioner is learning to become clay in the client's hands moulding to his or her needs. We become the therapist, with the specific tools, that he or she needs. It is imperative as newly practicing Art Therapists, that you do not find a new and exciting technique and 'try it out' on your next client. Learn all you can, continue to practice trusting in the process, and most of all be present for your client. Trust that if you are truly present and truly attentive, you will know when an opportunity presents. You will recognise just what he or she could use right now for insight or support.

As you worked through the experiential tasks in this text you may have found some worked better for you than others. The situations you brought to work with may not have been ideal for some of the tasks, or perhaps this simply was not a task to which you could relate. Sometimes a client will also appear not to have made any gains from an activity. That is fine. If the therapeutic relationship is sound, and the goal for therapy relevant and appropriate, then these less successful exercises will do no harm. You may even discover it is useful many sessions further along.

Remember not to use these exercises, or indeed any, slavishly. Each exercise can be adapted and carefully moulded to the client's circumstance and goal. When considering a task for a client, be sure, to ask yourself, "What do I hope my client will discover here?", "Is this in line with his or her goal for therapy?" and "Am I asking the right question or setting up the right expectation for this to happen?"

Therapy is an improvised art. You cannot know what your client will bring. You cannot prepare a 'tick-sheet' for therapy. All the books in the world cannot 'make' you an art therapist. First, you need to be an artist, a creator of your own world and art, familiar with the mediums and the ways in which they 'speak'. You will need to practice, continue to learn, believe in your profession and your capacity to do the work.

You must trust yourself, trust the art and most of all, trust your client to be his or her own best healer. You, importantly, carry the tools that he or she will use for the journey. And sometimes you are privileged to act as witness to the healing.

Bibliography

Bennett, L., & Wolin, S. (1984). Family Rituals. Family process , 401 - 420.

Bentham, J., & Harrison, R. E. (1988). Bentham: A Fragment on Government (Cambridge Texts in the History of Political Thought). Cambridge UK: Cambridge University Press.

Britannica, E. (n.d.). Dictionary. Retrieved January 21, 2012, from Miriam Webster Dictionary: http://www.merriam-webster.com/dictionary/habit?show=0&t=1327542566

Britta K Holzel, S. W.-O. (2011). How does Mindfulness Meditation Work? Proposing Mechanisms of Action from a Conceptual and Neural Perspective. Perspectives on Psychological Science 6 (6), 537 - 559.

Campbell, J. (1949). The Hero with a Thousand Faces 2nd Edition. Princeton University Press.

Campbell, J. (2008). The Hero with a Thousand Faces (The Collected Works of Joseph Campbell) 3rd Edition. California: New World Library.

Dalebroux, A., Goldstein, T. R., & Winner, E. (2008). Short-Term Mood Repair Through Art-Making: Positive Emotion is More Effective Than Venting. Motivation and Emotion , 32, 288 - 295.

De Petrillo, L., & Winner, E. (2005). Does Art Improve Mood? A Test of a Key Assumption Underlying Art Therapy. Journal of the American Art Therapy Association, , 22 (4), 205-212.

Faerna, J. M. (1995). Munch. New York: Harry N Abrahams.

Freud, S. (2010). The Interpretation of Dreams the Illustrated Edition Sterling Press . New York: Stirling Press.

Gazzaniga. (1998, 279). The split brain revisited. Scientific American , pp. 51-55.

Gazzaniga, M. (1998). The mind's past. Berkeley, CA: University of California Press.

H, L. (2009). Timing, timing, timing: Fast decoding of object information from intracranial field potentials in human visual cortex. . Neuron .

Henley, D. (2002). Clayworks in Art Therapy: Plying the Sacred Circle. UK: Jessica Kingsley.

Hinz, L. D. (2009). Expressive Therapies Continuum: A Framework for Using Art in Therapy. UK: Routledge.

Hobson, J., & McCarly, R. (1977). The brain as a dream-state generator: An activation-synthesis hypothesis of the dream process. American Journal of Psychiatry 134 (12) , 1335–1348.

Hudson, H. (Director). (1981 ). Chariots of Fire [Motion Picture].

J. A. Russell, A. W. (1989, 57). Affect grid: A single-item scale of pleasure and arousal. Journal of Personality and Social Psychology , 57 : p 493.

J. Azulaya, S. M. (25 October 2006). Influence of visual cues on gait in Parkinson's disease: Contribution to attention or sensory dependence? Dementia in Parkinson's Disease:

International Symposium (pp. Volume 248, Issues 1-2, Pages 192-195). Journal of the Neurological Sciences.

Jaffé, E. b. (1963). Memories, Dreams, Reflections Jung's autobiography. New York: Pantheon Books.

Jung, C. G. (1921). Psychological Types, or, The Psychology of Individuation. London: Kegan Paul Trench Trubner.

Jung, C. J. (1974). Dreams. Princeton NJ: Bollingen.

Jung, C. (1931). The Aims of Psychotherapy. In C. G. Jung, Collected Works 16: The Practice of Psychotherapy. (p. 86). London: Routledge.

Jung, C. (1999). The Essential Jung, second edition. (A. Storr, Ed.) Princeton, New Jersey: Princeton University Press.

Landy, R. (1996). Persona and Performance: The Meaning of Role in Drama, Therapy, and Everyday Life. New York: The Guilford Press.

Lewis, C. S. (1994). The Discarded Image. Cambridge UK: Cambridge University Press.

Little, D. (2008). What is hermeneutic explanation? Dearborn: University of Michigan.

M.P. Nichol, R. S. (2008). Family Therapy: Concepts and Methods (8th ed.). New York: Pearson Education.

McMillan, D. W. (2005). Emotion Rituals: A Resource for Therapists and Clients . London UK: Routledge.

Missildine, W. (1991). Your Inner Child of the Past (Later Edition). New York: Pocket.

Murdock, M. (1990). The Heroine's Journey. Boston: Shambhala.

Otto, R. (1989). Art and Artist: Creative Urge and Personality Development. (C. F. Atkinson, Trans.) New York: W.W. Norton and Company.

Prideaux, S. (2005). Edvard Munch: Behind the Scream. New Haven: Yale University Press.

Rank, O. (1922). Der Mythus von der Geburt des Helden. Leipzig: F. Deuticke.

Rank, Richter, & Lieberman. (2004). The Myth of the Birth of the Hero: A Psychological Exploration of Myth. Baltimore, Maryland: Johns Hopkins University Press.

Roberts, J. (1988). Setting the Frame, Definition, Functions and Typology of Rituals. In E. Imber-Black, J. Roberts, & R. A. Whiting, Rituals in Families and Family Therapy. New York: W.W. Norton.

Rogers, C. (1951). Client-Centered Therapy. Cambridge Massachusetts: The Riverside Press.

Rogers, C. (1961). On becoming a person. Boston USA: Houghton Mifflin.

Sara W. Lazar, C. E. (2005). Meditation experience is associated with increased cortical thickness. NeuroReport 16: Nov 28th , 1893-1897.

Sherwood, P. (2004). The Healing Art of Clay Therapy. Melbourne Au: Acer Press.

Turner, M. (1998). The Literary Mind. USA: Oxford University Press.

Unknown. The process of synaptic transmission in neurons. Alzheimers Publication Unraveling the Mystery. National Institute of Aging, USA.

Wegner, D. W. (2004). The Return of Suppressed Thoughts in Dreams. Psychological Science 15 (4) , 232 -236.